ZOROASTRIANISM

THE COMPLETE GUIDE ON THE ANCIENT PERSIAN RELIGION OF ZOROASTRIANISM

ALI HAKIMI

CONTENTS

INTRODUCTION 1

CHAPTER 1: What Is Zoroastrianism? 5

Religion In Iran Before Zoroastrianism 6

Beginnings Of Zoroastrianism 7

Zarathustra / Zoroaster 9

Zoroastrian Calendar 11

Day (Ruz, Roz, Roj) 12

Key Beliefs Of Zoroastrianism 20

Yasna 12 29

Practices 31

Chapter 2: Symbols, Sacred Sites, Scriptures, and Festivals. 40

Symbols 40

Sacred Sites 51

Scriptures 61

Festivals And Holy Days 70

Chapter 3: Ahura Mazda and Other Deities 84

Ahura Mazda 84

Spenta Mainyu (Holy Spirit) 86

Amesha Spentas 86

Angra Mainyu (Evil Spirit) 94

Chapter 4: History of the Religion 101

Timeline 101

Before Zoroastrianism 103

The Persian Empire 103

The Median Dynasty (Approximately Bce 678 – 549) 104

The Achaemenid Dynasty (Approximately Bce 549 – 329) 106

The Parthian Period (Approximately Bce 247 – Ce 224) 107

Sassanid Dynasty (Ce 224 – 651) 110

Muslim Conquest (Between Ce 633 – 651) 111

The Downfall Of Zoroastrianism 113

Abbasid Dynasty (Ce 752 – 804) 113

The Iranian Intermezzo/ Persian Renaissance (821 – 1055) 114

Mongols / Il-Khanid Dynasty (1256 – 1353) 124

The Timurid Empire And Ottoman Turks (1370 – 1508) 125

The Dynasty Of The Safavids (1500 - 1736) 128

The Afghan Interlude (1722 – 1730) 129

Nadir Shah (1736 – 1747) 130

The Dynasty Of The Zands (1751 – 1779) 133

The Dynasty Of The Qajars (1789 - 1925) 135

The Pahlavis And The Iranian Revolution (1925 – 1979) 137

The Islamic Republic Of Iran (1979-Present) 140

Migration To India (10th To 20th Centuries) 143

Persecution Of Zoroastrians 144

Offshoots Of Zoroastrianism 148

The Parsi-Muslim Riots 152

Chapter 5: What Is it Like Today? 155

Current Distribution Of Zoroastrians 155

Zoroastrian Influence On Popular Culture 157

Zoroastrianism In North America 160

Zoroastrian Groups And Associations In North America 161

Modern Zoroastrian Faith 165

Zoroastrian Values 167

World Zoroastrian Organization 171

World Zoroastrian Congress 172

World Zoroastrian Youth Congress 173

Chapter 6: Parsi and Zoroastrian Cuisine 175

Abgoosht – Chickpea And Lamb Soup 177

Akuri – Classic Parsi Eggs 178

Ash E Reshteh – Bean And Noodle Soup 178

Baghali Polo - Rice With Fava Beans And Dill 178

Chicken Farcha – Marinated Chicken 179

Dhansak Masala – Spice Mixture For Meats 179

Fesenjan – Stew Of Walnuts And Pomegranates 180

Gormeh Sabzi – Stew With Green Herbs 180

Haleem - Wheat And Meat Porridge 181

Jeweled Rice - Rice With Dried Fruit And Nuts 181

Kachubar – Cucumber And Tomato Salad 182

Kashk-E Bademjan - Eggplant Dip 182

Kebab – Ground Meat And Spices 183

Khichdi – Rice And Lentils 183

Khajoor Ni Ghari – Dates In Pastry 184

Khoresht-E Bademjan – Tomato And Eggplant Stew 184

Kolmi Papeto Tetralo – Prawns In Tomato Sauce 184

Lagan-Nu Custard – Custard For Weddings 185

Masoor Dal – Red Lentils 185

Paneer Cutlets – Vegetarian Cutlets 185

Parsi Mutton Cutlets 186

Parsi Sali Keema – Lamb Mince With Sali 186

Patra Ni Machi – Pomfret In Banana Leaves 186

Sadab – Ruta Leaves Fried With Bread 187

Sabzi Polo – Herbed Rice 187

Sabzi Khordan - Cheese And Herb Platter 188

Sali Boti – Mutton In Tomatoes 188

Sali Par Edu – Eggs And Potatoes 188

Sali Marghi – Masala Chicken 189

Shirin Polo – Sweet Rice Pilaf 189

Tahchin – Saffron Rice Layers 189

Tahdig - Crunchy Fried Rice 190

Zereshk Polo – Rice With Barberries 190

CONCLUSION 191

INTRODUCTION

Thank you for purchasing Zoroastrianism: The Complete Guide on the Ancient Persian Religion of Zoroastrianism. Whether you are new to Zoroastrianism or have some basic knowledge of the faith, we hope this book will deepen your knowledge and teach you something new about the first monotheistic religion known to exist.

For hundreds of years, Zoroastrianism predominated throughout the Persian Empire and is still followed in various regions of the world today. However, although it was once the most popular religion in the world, it is now relatively obscure. Within this book, you will find information about the birth of this old religion and how it is celebrated today. Zoroastrianism has popularized thousands of years ago, and many founding beliefs ultimately became the foundation for modern religions such as Christianity, Islam, and Judaism.

Zoroastrianism became popular in the Persian Empire when the population was very active on the world market and was highly respected. The power of the Persian Empire may have gone a long way toward spreading the religion at that time.

The basic tenants of Zoroastrianism may be familiar to modern people, but they were revolutionary in their day. You may not even know that these beliefs began with Zoroastrianism. The overriding belief of Zoroastrianism is in one God who created the world and rules over all creation. This monotheistic system contrasts with the previous system, where the people worshiped a pantheon of gods. Additionally, they think there is a never-ending conflict between the forces of good and evil and that it is our duty as humans to not only safeguard the world that God has endowed us with but also to oppose evil and make an effort to live morally upright lives. In addition to being a human responsibility, doing good deeds in this life will directly impact how you spend your eternity.

Within this book, you will find information regarding the creation of the religion, some of the central precepts of this religion, and how Zoroastrians celebrated their faith historically and today. You will also find some information about why and how its popularity declined and where you might still find some people practicing it today.

We will talk about how Zoroastrian people celebrate, and worship, including the scriptures they read, the celebrations they partake in, and information about some popular foods served for holidays and every day, including over 30 recipes for foods you might find at a Zoroastrian celebration.

Once again, I appreciate you choosing my book from the many available on the subject. So naturally, we attempted to pack it as full of information as possible.

A Prayer for the New Year

MIDDLE PERSIAN	ENGLISH
Az hamah gunah patet pashemanoom;	I repent from my misdeeds with sincere remorse;
Az harvastin duzhmata, duzhhukhta, duzhhvreshta mem pa geti	From every wicked idea, speech, or action I have ever had in this life,
Manid, oem goft, oem kard, oem jast, oem bun, bud ested;	whether they were spoken, done, or will be in the future;
Az an gunah manashni, gavashni, kunashni, tani ravani geti minoani,	from sins that were thought, said, or done to my body, to my soul, or to the corporeal world, and the spiritual world.
okhe avakh pasheman pa se gavashni, pa patetoom.	I acknowledge and repent, turning my back on them.

MIDDLE PERSIAN	ENGLISH
Khshnaothra Ahurahe Mazdao taroidite angra mainyeush;	In order to further the dominion of holy Ahura Mazda, the annihilation of the destructive spirit,
Haithya varshtanm hyat vasna fershotenem	and the accomplishment of good to create a brand new world.
Staomi Ashem.	I respect Asha.
Ashem Vohu, vahishtem asti, ushta asti.	Ashem Vohu is the greatest and represents eternal serenity.
Ushta ahmai, hyat ashai,	For those who chose goodness for its own sake, eternal peace is attained without expectation of reward
Vahishtai ashem.	The highest Asha is this.

CHAPTER 1
WHAT IS ZOROASTRIANISM?

Zoroastrianism is a monotheistic, equality-centered religion that is widely accepted to have originated about 4,000 years ago in Persia and is the world's oldest monotheistic religion. As a monotheistic religion, the believers only recognize one God rather than a pantheon or group of gods, as was seen in older religions in Greek or Latin areas. The earliest site archeologists can link to Zoroastrianism is a bronze age temple from the 2nd millennium BCE discovered in current-day Turkmenistan.

From 600 BCE to 650 CE, Zoroastrianism was the world's most prominent and widely-practiced religion. This theological system prevailed during the three great Persian Empires, the Achaemenid (BCE 550–330), the Parthian (BCE 247 – CE 224), and concluding with the Sasanian (CE 224 – 651), until Muslims conquered the region in the 7th century CE when Islam replaced it.

Their religious rights strongly feature fire, but they are not fire-worshippers, as some have mistakenly presumed. While worship generally takes place in a fire temple or Agiary, and many of the yearly festivals involve building a bonfire, the religion sees fire as a symbol of purity, representing the light of Ahura Mazda (God) and the mind in its illuminated state.

Today, there are two groups of Zoroastrians. One group in modern-day Iran, and the other, called Parsis, in modern-day northern India.

RELIGION IN IRAN BEFORE ZOROASTRIANISM

There are not a lot of reliable sources which tell us about the ancient religions in the area of modern-day Iran before the time that Zoroastrianism began to be popular. Much of the information about what existed before comes from the writings of the prophet Zarathustra. It describes ways in which Zoroastrianism differs from how the people worshiped before, without giving details since contemporaries of Zarathustra would already have this information.

Since the languages in Iran and northern India are similar, there were probably common ancestors who spoke an Indo-Aryan language in these areas. Moreover, sacred texts from both of these areas hint at polytheism and speak about gods with similar attributes, such as the Indian god Mitra and his Iranian counterpart Mithra, as well as the sacred quality of fire, among other things.

The Indo-Iranian people had different classes of gods, with the daeva or daeva being a more holy class with special powers available to them. At some point in history, there was a split between the people of India and the people of Iran because, in India, the daevas remained the highest form a god could take. At the same time, ahuras were considered demons, with their powers being menacing. However, the ahuras were the highest power in Iran, and the daevas had the rank of demons. Not all of this comes from the teachings of Zarathustra. Some differences point toward a significant split between these groups in the past, which historians have not uncovered.

BEGINNINGS OF ZOROASTRIANISM

Zoroastrianism developed amongst wandering tribes that eventually established communities in the areas of northern India and modern-day Iran. The commonly acknowledged birthplace of Zoroastrianism was somewhere around the Helmand Basin in the Sistan region along the present-day borders of Iran and Afghanistan. The religion shares some common history with the Vedic religion from India and Hinduism, with the significant difference being the monotheistic nature of Zoroastrianism.

Many academics argue that the Zoroastrian principles influenced the development of many other monotheistic religions, including Islam, Judaism, and Christianity, due to the Persian Empire's global dominance. But Zoroastrianism predated all examples of these religions that are known to have existed. Since all of them share several features in common, it appears that they all were heavily interested in Zoroastrianism. For example, in 539 BCE, Cyrus conquered Babylon and liberated the Babylonian Jews. Many of the Jews took the ideas of their liberators with them when they returned home to Jerusalem. Among those ideas were the tenants of Zoroastrianism, used when creating the Hebrew Bible.

Zoroastrians believe in one God, Ahura Mazda (or Ahuramazda). Although Zoroastrianism was not insistent or unwavering in its promotion of a single deity, it is the first documented attempt at unifying the worship of the people and directing it towards one deity rather than a pantheon of gods and goddesses as seen in other early peoples.

Aside from being one of the first monotheistic religions, Zoroastrianism promotes the concept of duality amongst the believers. In Zoroastrianism, the duality of the world teaches that there are two basic and opposing principles in everything, the good and the bad. This duality of good and evil is true of people, situations, places, animals, and every other aspect of life. The goal of practitioners of Zoroastrianism is to seek to increase the good in themselves and decrease the evil, thus bringing them closer to Heaven. Only those in which the good outweighs the evil will be able to enter paradise in the afterlife. Therefore, many festivals and ceremonies in Zoroastrianism focus on ridding oneself of any evil deeds, thoughts, or words which may have accumulated.

The dualism that Zoroastrianism embraces was never promoted as heavily in other religions but remained one of the central tenants of Zoroastrianism. Good and evil are in a constant battle within each person. Therefore, everyone must strive toward the good and away from the evil. Those who remain on the side of good can reap the rewards that await them after death in Heaven or paradise. This way, Zoroastrianism trained the people to value ethics and optimism even through hardship.

Since Zoroastrians believed in a duality of all things, the opposite of Ahura Mazda is Angra Mainyu, translated as 'destructive spirit.' He embodies death and is the source of all the evil in the world. Where Ahura Mazda is a faultless being who lives in Heaven with those worthy, Angra Mainyu lives in Hell with those who deserve eternal punishment. Like many religions that came afterward, when a person dies, they will have their deeds measured. Ahura Mazda will send the person's soul to spend eternity in either Heaven or Hell. Each person's fate is determined based on their good or evil deeds while they lived on Earth. The concepts of Heaven, hell, God, and the Devil in Christianity, Judaism, and Islam were all heavily influenced by Zoroastrianism.

ZARATHUSTRA / ZOROASTER

The religion of Zoroastrianism began because of the teachings of the prophet Zarathustra. He is known outside of Iran by the name Zoroaster, the Greek translation of his name.

Prophet Zarathustra was descended from the Spitaman family. Although most of his past is unknown, the Avesta, a holy text, contains some information about him. Although some place Zoroaster's existence as early as 1500 BCE, the traditional chronology places it in the 6th century BCE, when Cyrus the Great ruled the Persian Empire. Many believe that he was born and raised somewhere in northern Iran or southern Afghanistan and that he likely coexisted with a group of believers in Hinduism or another related religion. The first known accounts of a prophet—someone who receives direct revelation from God and uses that information to instruct the populace—come from Zarathustra.

Zarathustra was constantly curious about what was happening around him and spent much time outside as a child. He was incredibly bright and active. He was renowned for frequently challenging the professors and priests. According to a legend, the head priest of his community invited him to sit and converse with him as a little boy. He questioned the priest while there and even had some answers that confused him. Unfortunately, the priest allegedly suffered a heart attack and passed away after Zarathustra left.

Zarathustra decided to leave his home at the age of twenty to seek out the truth of life. It is thought that he became "illuminated" while seeking the truth. This illumination allegedly occurred when Zarathustra encountered Vohu Mana, an angel, and began to believe in Ahura Mazda as the one true God. During his life, he also married a woman named Hvovi and had six children. The family of Zarathustra was among the first to adopt the religion that is now known as Zoroastrianism.

The stories tell of a man who had a vision at 30 years old. He was bathing in a river during a religious celebration. He saw a being made of pure, white light standing just above him on the bank of the river. This individual introduced himself as Vohu Mana, meaning Good Mind. Vohu Mana led Zarathustra down a path to meet Ahura Mazda, who was sitting alongside five other beings called Amesha Spentas (the Holy Immortals). After this first encounter, Zarathustra visited Ahura Mazda and the Amesha Spentas several times and spent long hours speaking with them about good and evil. The conversations that they held form the basis of the Zoroastrian religion.

Although Ahura Mazda is the one true God in Zoroastrianism, there is some acknowledgment of other divine entities such as the Amesha Spentas since in one of Zarathustra's hymns, he mentions that Mazda resides along with other ahuras. These divine beings are not worshipped as gods but are more like godly counsel or are supporters of Ahura Mazda. In other contemporary documents, people are worshipping Ahura Mazda alongside other godly figures or worshipping Ahura Mazda as the king of the gods. The appearance of other holy deities suggests an extended transition period from a polytheistic system to a monotheistic attitude where Ahura Mazda is God.

There are no contemporary writings about Zarathustra outside the holy books associated with Zoroastrianism. He is believed to have been a priest of a particular ahura named Mazda, or wise, during a time when the area recognized many gods. Zarathustra was the first to suggest that there is only one God, and the rest of the immortal beings are his supporters.

Historians have found it challenging to place the hymns or Gathas of Zarathustra into historical context since no people or places are mentioned in the documents that can pinpoint a specific time or place. All that is known is that he lived somewhere in the east of present-day Iran before the empire combined under Cyrus the Great. He is not directly mentioned in contemporary documents, but he has been credited with instructing Pythagoras and inspiring the Chaldean doctrines that speak of astrology and magic. These things cannot be confirmed, however. The teachings of Zarathustra appear to have reached western Iran by around 350 BCE since some of Aristotle's works written at this time allude to the dualism of the religion in Persia.

ZOROASTRIAN CALENDAR

Zoroastrian calendars have names for each month and day and specific periods within the day. A Zoroastrian year consists of exactly 12 months, each with 30 days, for a total of 360 days, and each day is further divided into five watches.

In the Zoroastrian calendar, each month and day is named for and dedicated to a particular deity or concept of divinity. Since the prayers include the names of the days and months, calendar dedications have significant religious importance. The ongoing recitation of the names of the primary deities establishes their hierarchy. For instance, the six months are named after the Amesha Septas, whereas the one month, Dey, often known as "Creator," is named after Ahura Mazda. The following months have names that are based on religious principles.

MONTH	DEDICATED TO:
1. Farvardin	Farevashi
2. Ordibeshesht	Asha Vahishta
3. Kordad	Haurvatat
4. Tir	Tishtrya
5. Amordad	Ameretat
6. Sahrivar	Khastra Vairya
7. Mehr	Mitrah
8. Aban	Ap
9. Azar	Atar /Adur
10. Dey	Ahura Mazda
11. Bahman	Vohu Mana
12. Asfand	Spenta Armaiti

DAY (RUZ, ROZ, ROJ)

Each day of the month is named after a divine being or a divine concept to which it is dedicated. Each ritual is planned to correspond to a complementary day during the month. Naming each day of the month establishes the hierarchy of significant divinities and guarantees that the people will invoke each of these essential beings or concepts frequently since both the day and the month are mentioned during religious ceremonies and every act of worship. Evidence for the presence of daily dedications comes from Yasna 16 and the Siroza, another Avesta text. Yasna 16, one of the prayers in the scriptures, is primarily an adoration of the divinities with day dedications. This document has the earliest (albeit undateable) documentation for the existence of these daily dedications, and the first place that the names appear in this order is in those Avestan language verses:

MONTH	DEDICATED TO:
1. Dadvah Ahura Mazda	Creator Lord Mazda
2. Vohu Mana	Good Thought
3. Asa Vahista	Best Truth
4. Khsathra Vaiyra	Desirable Dominion
5. Spenta Armaiti	Holy Devotion
6. Harvatat	Wholeness
7. Ameretat	Immortality
8. Davadah Ahura Mazda	Creator Lord Mazda
9. Atar	Fire
10. Apo	Waters
11. Hvar Khshaeta	Sun
12. Mah	Moon

MONTH	DEDICATED TO:
13. Tistrya	Stars, Heavens
14. Geus Urvan	Animal Creation
15. Dadvah Ahura Mazda	Creator Lord Mazda
16. Mithra	Contracts, Love
17. Sraosha	Hearkening
18. Rashnu	Justice
19. Fravasayo	Progress Force
20. Verthraghna	Victory
21. Raman	Peace, Happiness
22. Vata	Wind, Breath of Life
23. Dadvah Ahura Mazda	Creator Lord Mazda
24. Daena	Inner Vision
25. Ahsi	Recompense
26. Arshtat	Justice, Truth
27. Asman	Sky
28. Zam	Earth
29. Mantra Spenda	Holy Word
30. Anagranam Raochangha	Endless Light

Days two through seven are dedicated to those closest to Ahura Mazda, the Amesha Spentas. These are the divine counsel of Ahura

Mazda, the six divine sparks. These are the angels who helped Ahura Mazda to create the world. These divine sparks are known as the archangels in modern Zoroastrianism who were responsible for the completion of all subsequent creations.

Days nine through 13 are dedicated to five sacred prayers in the scriptures which speak of the moon, the sun, the elements of water and fire, and titrya, which may here serve as a metaphor for the entire heavenly sphere. Day 14 is for animal creation. Often the symbol for all animals is the ox.

The second half of the month begins on day 16, which is dedicated to the divinity of oaths and contracts by recognizing the Great Mithra. On days 17–22, the ones closest to Mithra, the judges of the soul are honored. The Fravashi, Fravasayo, Verthraghna, Raman, and Vata are the successors of Sraosha and Rashnu.

Finally, are the recognitions of inner vision or religion, recompense, justice, the sky, the earth, the Holy Word, and endless light. These are the more abstract concepts but are important in the Zoroastrian faith and worthy of continual recognition.

There are four days each month devoted just to Ahura Mazda. There is contradicting literature on the matter, and having four days set apart for Ahura Mazda is something that has been discussed for ages. The eighth, sixteenth, and twenty-third days of the calendar may have previously been devoted to different deities. Probably, the agreement between orthodox and heterodox organizations to observe Ahura Mazda for four days came about initially. Based on a similar Egyptian practice, the practice of having specific dieties rule over each day of the month was first begun at some point around 400 BCE, most likely under Artaxerxes II (404 – 358 BCE).

Watch (Gah or Geh)

Five watches, each beginning at dawn, divided a 24-hour day before the development of modern timekeeping:

- ➤ Hawan (lasting from sunrise until noon)
- ➤ Second Hawan or Rapithwin (from noon until 3 pm)
- ➤ The Uzerin (from 3 pm until sunset)
- ➤ The Aiwisruthrem (from sunset until midnight)
- ➤ The Ushahin (from midnight until sunrise)

Rapithwin, according to some academics, was only added in the Middle Ages. However, some documents show that Hawan lasted from sunrise until three in the afternoon before that time.

The Calendar

The 360-day calendar, which everyone widely used from at least the middle of the 5th century BCE, was based on earlier calendars before the Sassanid ruler Ardashir I's reform (226 - 241 CE). Since the actual duration of the Earth's rotation is 365¼ days, that system involved periodically adding a thirteenth month to the calendar to make up for the shortfall that had built up over time.

The 365-day calendar that the Egyptian calendar much more closely modeled Ardashir I instituted. The names remained the same throughout the Achaemenid Empire, although they persisted for 12 months of 30 days each. To comply with the new calendar pattern, the priests added five days to the end of the 12th month each year. These five intercalary days, known as Gatha or Gah days, were thought to occur outside of the calendar year and were so named after hymns from the earlier Avesta.

After giving up on intercalation, everyone decided that the first day of the ninth month would mark the start of the new year. Due to confusion and disagreement about the new system, many Zoroastrian feasts and holidays had two dates and still do; some Zoroastrians still adhere to this tradition. To ensure that nobody misses the holy days, priests performed various rites across several days rather than just one.

Another change to the calendar was adopted by Hormizd I in 272 CE due to the situation becoming too convoluted. He created the continuous six-day feasts by joining the new and old holy days. The only exception to this rule was Nowroz, or new year, on the spring equinox. This holiday remained a five-day festival, and the sixth day was celebrated as the birthday of Zarathustra.

By the time Yazdegerd III (who ruled from 632 to 651) came into power, the calendar and seasons were four months off because there had been no intercalation since Ardashir I had abolished the practice of intercalculation. As a result, the Gahambars (the seasonal feasts) were at the wrong time of the year. Moreover, further reforms that Yazdegerd III had planned were not implemented because the Muslim invasion toppled the monarchy.

The Seleucids (312-248 BCE) proposed dating by era, as was the Hellenic custom, as opposed to naming years according to the reign of kings, and so named the era the Alexandrian era after he conquered Persia in 330 BCE (this period is now called the Seleucid era). However, the Zoroastrian priests disagreed with this method, so they created a new era called the Zoroastrian era, which also gave rise to the first serious attempt to discover the accurate birth year of Zarathustra.

Following the Seleucids, the Parthians (150 BCE – 224 CE) celebrated the tradition of naming years. It wasn't until Ardashir I's calendar reform that dates according to the king's rule was reinstated. The modern Zoroastrian calendar will often include a Y.Z. suffix to denote the calendar era or the numbering system used to create the calendar. Typically, the calendars are dated beginning with Yazdegerd III, the final Sassanian king crowned in 632 CE.

The calendar and the seasons gradually became out of sync due to the lack of intercalation in Ardashir I's calendar changes. The Zoroastrian theologian Zadspram had already recognized the less-than-ideal situation in the 9th century and predicted that the two systems would be four years out of sync at the Final Judgement.

The vernal equinox fell on New Year's Day in 1006 once more, and (according to mythology) the decision was made that the official Zoroastrian calendar would add an extra month of 30 days every 120 years to try and keep the calendars more harmonized. This extra month, known as Aspandarmad vahizak, was added by Parsi people living in India between 1125 and 1250. However, since subsequent Parsi generations either neglected or forgot to intercalate the thirteenth month, that month would also be the last one to do so. The calendar was known as the Shahenshahi (imperial) calendar when it was decided to intercalate every 120 years. The Parsis continued to refer to their calendar as Shahenshahi since they were unaware they were not intercalating properly. Even now, this custom is still used, and supporters of other Zoroastrian calendar systems disparage the Shahenshahi as "royalist."

Around 1720, Jamasp Peshotan Velati, a Zoroastrian priest Iran to India. When he arrived, he discovered a discrepancy between his calendar and the Parsi calendar. This discrepancy was brought to the priests of Surat, but nobody could agree which calendar was correct.

Some powerful priests claimed that their visitor's calendar version must be accurate since he was from the ancient homeland. As a result, many Parsis in and around Surat changed their calendars on June 6th, 1745, following the advice of their priests. The Kadimi calendar, also known as Kadmi or Quadmi, originated in Iran and India.

The "Zarthosti Fasili Sal Mandal," also known as the Zoroastrian Seasonal-Year Society, was founded in 1906 by Bombay Parsi Khurshedji Cama. This calendar came to be known as the Fasili calendar. It was based on an earlier version that had been adopted well in rural villages when it was introduced during the rule of the Seljuk Malik Shah in approximately 1079.

This calendar's standout features are as follows:

1) The spring equinox and New Year's Day coincided with the passing of the seasons.

2) The year consists of 12 months, each of which has 30 days, with an additional five days at the conclusion.

3) After the five Gah days, the calendar added a leap day every four years.

The Fasli organization argued that their calendar was correct and that the other two were merely political.

The new seasonal calendar, which they called the Bastani calendar, was first not well received by the Indian Zoroastrian community. Still, after a drive in 1930 to persuade Zoroastrians living in Iran to accept it, the Fasli calendar started to gain favor in Iran. Combining them was easy because the Iranian calendar still used Zoroastrian names for the months. In 1935, independent of the Fasli movement, the Iranian Parliament approved a new calendar that embraced the points offered by the Fasili Society. The majority of Zoroastrians duly embraced the Bastani calendar. However, the Zoroastrian community in Yazd resisted and still uses the Kadmi calendar today.

All three calendars lined up again in 1992, but despite many Zoroastrians' suggestions to combine the calendars, no one could agree on which calendar to adopt. Additionally, some priests opposed it because re-consecrating the sacred objects would be costly.

KEY BELIEFS OF ZOROASTRIANISM

The Zoroastrian faith consists of a core of central beliefs. They hold that there is a single God, he is all-powerful, a dualistic reality, that all creation is divine, and that everything in the universe and everyone is spiritual. All Zoroastrians are expected to:

> Proclaim your steadfast devotion to Ahura Mazda.
> Aspire to the admirable traits of Amesha Spentas.
> Believe in the holiness and divinity of Ahura Mazda's creation.
> Altogether reject and discourage evil in your life.
> Practice fostering excellent ideas, words, and acts.
> Adhere to Zoroaster's and the teachers' instructions.
> Commit to living righteously.

Belief in a Supreme and Universal God

Zoroastrianism preaches belief in a single God, Ahura Mazda, or Wise Lord. This divine being is supreme, omnipotent, and omniscient. He symbolizes truth, radiance, strength, and patience and protects the good from chaotic evil by maintaining order in the world. The kind and just Ahura Mazda created the universe.

Ahura Mazda is:

- ➢ Omnipotent (all-powerful)
- ➢ Unchanging
- ➢ The Source of all goodness and happiness
- ➢ Omniscient (knows everything)
- ➢ The Creator of life
- ➢ Omnipresent (is everywhere)
- ➢ Impossible for humans to conceive

God is supreme. According to Zoroastrian teachings, everything in the universe is pure. Hence it ought to be loved and respected. Zoroastrian adherents traditionally refrain from polluting rivers, land, or the atmosphere because they believe land, water, and air deserve respect. Some view Zoroastrianism as the first ecological religion because of this reverence.

While Ahura Mazda is supreme, Zoroastrians also recognize other divinities that exist but are not equal to Ahura Mazda. The main divinities are the six Amesha Spentas or Immortal Beings, who personify the excellent qualities of Ahura Mazda. Under these are angels, ahuras, and other divinities. Rituals may be performed for any divinities, and many have a day of the month devoted to them, during which they are mentioned in prayers and religious rites. Each divine being has a domain they govern, and Ahura Mazda oversees all.

Acceptance of Sin and Forgiveness of Sin

According to Zoroastrians, wickedness defiles the environment and puts people in danger. Therefore, indulging in sinful activities is forbidden. Theft, adultery, sodomy, pollution of the environment, touching dead animals or people, practicing other faiths, not performing prayers and rituals to Ahura Mazda, and not disposing of the dead following the prescribed method are all examples of sin. Sin can also result from not adhering to God's religious instructions or not practicing the three commandments given to Zarathustra by Ahura Mazda for the people to follow: practice good thoughts, good deeds, and good words. Any transgression of the commandments, including harboring wicked thoughts or engaging in commerce with malice aforethought, would be unacceptable. The scriptures also outline the steps that must be taken to make up for specific sins, while it recommends death as the appropriate punishment for some grave offenses. Zoroastrian literature spends some time outlining the sins that will result in punishment.

Conviction in the Divinity of Creation

Zoroastrians acknowledged that Ahura Mazda established and constructed the world for humans. The conflict between the forces of good and evil, and ultimately the victory of the forces of good, is made possible by the world's existence. Ahura Mazda, being omniscient, knew that good would eventually win over evil. Everyone is accountable for maintaining the purity and keeping the order that Ahura Mazda established because God created everything.

The Duality of Existence

Zoroastrians believe that our world has a prominent dichotomy between good and evil. Zoroastrianism is the original dualistic world view, describing the world in terms of good and evil. Following this view, there will be a final victory against evil on Earth in the end. This belief also allows for the concepts of heaven, hell, the afterlife, and a day of judgment for all individuals. Like many modern religions, each person's experiences of the afterlife are determined by their actions and choices made during their life.

Although Zoroastrianism is a monotheistic religion, some deities from older religions have been incorporated as lesser deities that are often described as either angels or demons, depending on whether they support the good or the evil.

Every Zoroastrian within the society is accountable for preserving and developing the purity of existence by abstaining from evil. Everyone can improve the good by adhering to Zarathustra's ideas and engaging in religious rituals and observances. The choice for believers is between right and wrong. A person can cross the bridge to heaven if, when they pass away, their good deeds outweigh their harmful deeds. On the other hand, they will plunge off the bridge and into hell if their sins outweigh their good.

Belief in the Holiness of the Elements

The spiritual world was created before the material world by Ahura Mazda. Evil cannot penetrate or contaminate the spiritual world since it is outside of its realm of influence. However, humans should be aware of the risks that arise in the world while avoiding being influenced by evil forces because the material world is not immune to evil. People are advised to refrain from taking any actions that can contaminate physical objects, such as the elements of fire, water, earth, and air. Pollution is a sign of evil entering an element. Leading a life that is righteous and avoiding contact with dead things is one of the ways that humans can prevent pollution. Avoiding contact with the dead is also why they believe that dead bodies should not be buried in the ground or thrown in the water, as this can cause pollution or contamination of the element. Zoroastrians practice sky burial, where vultures and other carrion animals dispose of their bodies. They claim that God mainly designed these creatures for this function.

A Conviction of the Significance of Righteousness

According to the Zoroastrian worldview, the world is where the forces of good and evil battle. The primary duty of a human is to assist Ahura Mazda in removing evil from the world forever by strongly supporting goodness. Therefore, men should try to uphold Asha, also known as order, truth, and good behavior, everywhere they go. In addition, men and women are tasked with nurturing within themselves the qualities embodied in the six Immortal Beings.

Belief in the Spirituality of People and the World

The world consists of spiritual beings and phenomena that Ahura Mazda created utilizing his spiritual energy. The world's elements—fire, water, air, earth, plants, animals, and people—represent the body of God, whose spirit sustains everything. Therefore, humans must respect and cherish the world because it and everything in it are products of God's spiritual essence.

Belief in Prophets

The teachings of the prophet Zarathustra, commonly known as the first prophet, serve as the foundation for the entire Zoroastrian religion. Zarathustra received the instructions for this new religion in a vision, and it was through him that the populace received guidance on how to follow the righteous path. Everyone can learn the first prophet's teachings by reading the Avesta. According to Zoroastrians, the birth of Zarathustra marked the start of a 3000-year creation cycle. They believe that a new prophet would appear to preserve Zarathustra's teachings and guide Zoroastrians for the next 1000 years at the end of each millennium of this cycle. According to Zoroastrian beliefs, the third prophet will be Shoshyant, a descendant of Zarathustra. His birth will announce Judgement Day and the destruction of all evil forces in the physical realm.

Beliefs Regarding the Afterlife

The Zoroastrian faith teaches that the physical world is polluted by evil, which causes death and decay because of Angira Mainyu and his determination to spread evil. The presence of evil is something that Ahura Mazda allowed on the condition that the evil was confined and would eventually be destroyed by the good.

While a person is alive, they are filled with the Spirit of God. They, therefore, cannot be corrupted by Angira Mainyu since Angira Mainyu is not strong enough to destroy the spirit, made of the same material as God. When a person dies, their spirit leaves the body behind, and then Angira Mainyu can enter the body and cause it to decay. Because of the presence of evil after death, Zoroastrian tradition dictates that dead bodies must be kept separate. Families or priests should remove the bodies of the dead to a dakhma or sky temple as soon as possible. Physically separating the bodies will save bystanders from the influence of this evil. Anyone touching a corpse intentionally or unintentionally is a mortal sin and could result in the death penalty in ancient times.

Upon death, the spirit or soul of a person leaves the body but remains in the area for three days and nights. Frequently, the spirit suffers from anxiety and distress because of its separation from its body. While the spirit is waiting and adjusting to the new reality, the archangel Vohuman and Mithra, the immortal in charge of the rising sun, oaths, and justice, consider the balance of good and evil present in the soul. On the third night after death, the spirit officially leaves the material world and is led by the angel Daena to the Chinawad Bridge, also called the Bridge of Judgement. As the spirit crosses the bridge, the person's deeds while alive are reviewed. If the person's deeds are determined to be on the side of good, they are led across a wide, paved bridge by angels through sweet-scented blossoms and into the pure light towards Paradise. If the person's deeds are evil, they will find that they walk on a narrow, creaking bridge with razor-thin beams that cut the feet. They will pass through thickets of thorns before being pushed off the bridge towards Hell and a place of punishment.

Some Zoroastrians believe that spirits are born onto the Earth to overcome some defects and to achieve perfection. This is similar to the idea of reincarnation, although reincarnation is not part of the Zoroastrian belief system. Therefore, each person's life on Earth is an opportunity to achieve perfection and become a perfect being of life. Entering Heaven or Hell is not the end of the journey for the spirit. They will remain in either Heaven or Hell until the end of the current cycle of time, when there will be Judgment Day, and Ahura Mazda will revive all the dead souls and review their actions again. At that point, Ahura Mazda will determine whether the spirit should remain in Heaven or Hell for eternity.

As an extension of the theme of duality throughout Zoroastrianism, Heaven and Hell are opposite. As described in the scriptures, Heaven is an enjoyable place filled with comfort, light, and the presence of Ahura Mazda and the immortals. At the same time, Hell is a very dark cave filled with chaos, pain, and filth where Angira Mainyu takes pleasure in torturing souls.

Heaven and Hell were new concepts at the time of Zoroastrianism, which emphasized the importance of the duality of the religion.

Everything was black and white, good and evil, and for a person to gain access to Paradise, it was vitally important to lead a selfless and good life.

According to Zoroastrian tradition, the universe has a lifespan of 12,000 years. Judgement Day will happen at the end of these 12,000 years. Zoroastrians believe that when the current cycle of 3000 years ends, Ahura Mazda will destroy evil in the final battle and proclaim the Day of Judgment. The deceased will all rise at this point and look back on their lives once more. Under his instructions, those who demonstrate their religiosity and loyalty will be appropriately rewarded with an eternity in Heaven. At the same time, the remainder of the populace will be sentenced to an eternity in Hell.

The Infinite Time is the name given to the first phase. Ahura Mazda existed at this time and was eternal. He was the illimitable, all-knowing, righteous, and eternal light. He was alone and lived in the area of brightness. Angra Septa, the terrible being, was currently in his shadowy realm. He was never-ending darkness, motivated by malice and destructive ambition. They were divided by a vast Void, or what some refer to as ether.

Both are referred to as finite and infinite. From the lofty heights of the light area above, Ahura Mazda is infinite or endless, and Angra Septa is infinite or endless from the pitiless depths of the darkness below.

However, both are seen as finite since they are separated from one another and constrained by the void. Since God Ahura Mazda is omniscient, He was aware of Angra Septa's existence beyond the void from the beginning, but Angra Septa was unaware of Ahura Mazda. Nevertheless, because Ahura Mazda knew about the upcoming conflict between the two of them, he spiritually formed several beings to help him.

At some point, Angra Mainyu rose from his dark place and came into the bright and star-filled domain of Ahura Mazda. Upon seeing the bright domain, he was overcome with a desire to destroy and so wanted to attack but could not defeat Ahura Mazda and the beings he had created. Ahura Mazda knew that a great battle would result and offered Angra Mainyu peace if he obeyed his commands and respected the creatures of light. Unfortunately, Angra Mainyu didn't understand that the offer was a peace offering and rejected the offer thinking that Ahura Mazda was weak.

Ahura Mazda agreed with Angra Mainyu to defer the coming battle for 9000 years. During the 9000-year break, Ahura Mazda knew that he would retain control of the universe for the first 3000 years and that he would be able to maintain the balance of good and evil during the next 3000 years. In the final 3000 years, he would render the Evil Spirit useless. Angra Mainyu accepted the agreement and fell back into his dark domain for 3000 years, during which time both he and Ahura Mazda built up their domains and gathered followers.

The fourth period, the last 3000 of the 12,000 years of the universe, is the period in which we live. It began with the birth of Zarathustra, and during this period, a new Saviour will appear at the end of each Millenium. Finally, the last Saviour will be Saoshyant, a descendant of Zarathustra, and he will wage a battle against the evil forces and set in motion the events that will end with Judgement Day.

YASNA 12

The Avesta's Yasna 12—which is transcribed below—mentions the essential tenets of the Zoroastrian creed.

Allegiance and Devotion to God

1. I detest Daevas. I identify as a Mazda-worshipper, a Zarathushtra supporter, a Daeva-hater, a fan of Ahura's doctrine, a praiser of the Amesha Spentas, and an Amesha Spentas worshipper. Nevertheless, I attribute all good to Ahura Mazda, together with all that is Asha-endowed, beautiful, and xwarena-endowed. Ahura Mazda is the source of the cow, Asha, and light; may this light illuminate the domains of his happiness.

2. Let the good Spenta Armaiti be mine; she is who I chose. I abjure cow stealing, robbery, and destroying and pillaging Mazdayasnian communities.

3. I want homesteaders and people who live on this planet with their cattle to have the ability to travel and live anywhere they please. Therefore, I make the following pledge in homage to Asha and with gifts: I will never again destroy or pillage the Mazdayasnian towns, even at the risk of my life.

Rejection of Evil According to the Teachings of Zarathustra

4. I discard the rule of the Daevas, the evilest beings, and the most destructive beings. They are wicked, no-good, lawless, and evil-knowing. I reject the Daevas and their allies, the yatu (demons) and their allies, and everyone who hurts living things. I reject them through my words, actions, and ideas. I openly reject them.

I reject the head authorities and the antagonistic druj followers at the same time.

5. As Ahura Mazda instructed Zarathushtra during all conversations, meetings, and gatherings where Mazda and Zarathushtra spoke;

6. In the same way that Zarathushtra, the Asha-endowed Zarathushtra, denied the power of the Daevas, I, a supporter of Zarathushtra and a Mazda-worshipper, deny the power of the Daevas.

Belief in the Sanctity and Divinity of the World

7. I am a Mazda-worshipper of this belief and teaching. Just as I believe in the waters, the plants, and the well-made Original Cow; as I believe in Ahura Mazda, who created the Cow and the Asha-endowed Man; as I believe in Zarathushtra, Kavi Vishtaspa, Frashaostra, and Jamaspa; as I believe in each of the Saoshyants (saviors).

Pledge to Follow the Three Commandments

8. I have promised and declared that I am a Zoroastrian who worships the god Mazda. I reaffirm my commitment to the well-considered idea, the well-spoken word, and the well-executed action.

Declaration of Faith

9. I swear allegiance to the Mazdayasnian religion, which commands the laying down of weapons and the postponement of attacks; it upholds khvaetvadatha, Asha-endowed; and it is the most incredible, best, and most beautiful of all religions that are or will

be: Zoroastrian, or Ahuric. I credit Ahura Mazda with all good. This is the Mazdayasnian religion's creed.

PRACTICES

Numerous particular rituals, sacrifices, festivals, and services are part of the Zoroastrian religion. However, Zarathustra was known to have believed in minimizing the significance of rituals and emphasizing the Threefold Path's core ethics of "Good Words, Good Thoughts, and Good Deeds." Living correctly in day-to-day life is more important than participating in rituals and ceremonies. According to the Zoroastrian religion, one must actively and morally engage in life by doing good deeds resulting in good thoughts and words. Living life in this way will ensure happiness and prevent chaos. While historically allowing for mild displays of these beliefs, Zoroastrianism as a religion prohibits extreme forms of austerity and monasticism. This active involvement is a crucial feature of Zoroaster's theory of free will.

Life is a transient state in Zoroastrian tradition and is merely the beginning of the life cycle. Accordingly, Zoroastrian people must actively take part in the ongoing struggle between the truth (Asha) and lies while they are still living (Druj). Since Ahura Mazda created the universe, a person's urvan (soul) has been without end and linked to their fravashi (personal / higher spirit). Therefore, before the urvan separates, the fravashi participates in Ahura Mazda's maintenance of the created world. The fravashi serves as both a spiritual protector and a source of inspiration for a person throughout their lifetime. When things get tough, the living can draw upon ancestors' cultural, spiritual, and brave fravashis tied to illustrious bloodlines to help them. The urvan and the fravashi are reunited on the fourth day after death. At this time, the memories of existence in the physical world are reviewed.

These encounters are judged based on the balance of good versus evil during the person's life and their spiritual struggle for goodness. Zoroastrianism does not often embrace the idea of rebirth. However, there have been numerous theological declarations in support of vegetarianism throughout Zoroastrianism's history, as well as assertions that Zoroaster was a vegetarian.

Religious activities strongly emphasize purification and reinforce it at every stage of life. In Zoroastrianism, the agents of ceremonial purity are water (aban) and fire (atar). Believers consider the cleansing ceremonies associated with fire and water connected with life's essence. According to scripture, the fire began in the waters, suggesting that water and fire are the second and third essential components generated in Zoroastrian cosmology. Fire and water are considered necessary for life near fire temples. As fire is present in all light sources, Zoroastrians pray close to it. They strengthen the waters as the last step in their principal act of worship. Water is supposed to be the source of spiritual insight, whereas fire is the main conduit via which believers can attain spiritual awareness. Therefore, the people praise the Yazatas Atar and Anahita; the subjects of litanies and praise hymns are water and fire, respectively.

Zoroastrianism does not dictate how people worship. Followers choose how and when they pray. There are other occasions for worshipers to congregate, such as the Navjote. The Navjote is an initiation rite for children of both sexes, where they are ritually purified and admitted into the Zoroastrian fellowship. Seasonal festivals, of which Zoroastrians have several, are communal affairs.

The Parsis from the Indian subcontinents and Iranian Zoroastrians have not proselytized or sought to convert others since at least the 18th century due to various social and political reasons. The Revayats and other scriptures reinforce the historical opinion of Zoroastrian high priests that there is no reason to forbid conversion, which later priests denounced. Many oppressed Zoroastrians in Iran have historically opposed conversion or have not given it much thought in practice. Although the highest ecclesiastical authority in Iran, the Council of Tehran Mobeds, now supports conversion, it is against the law to convert from Islam to Zoroastrianism following Iranian law.

Prayers

Zoroastrians typically offer their prayers multiple times per day. Some people wear kustis, which are cords that have been triple-knotted, as a reminder of the proverb "Good Words, Good Thoughts, Good Deeds." First, they encircle the sudreh, a long, spotless white cotton shirt, with the kusti. Then, they would untie and retie it while praying after engaging in a purification ritual, such as washing their hands.

Most prayers are thank-and-praise statements that honor Ahura Mazda and his glorious essence, penetrating everything. Prayers are recited while facing the sun, a fire, or a light source to invoke Ahura Mazda's divine force and light.

Zoroastrian rites place a heavy emphasis on purification. Zoroastrians strongly emphasize keeping their surroundings, bodies, and minds clean to fight evil (Angra Mainyu). Fire is regarded as the ultimate symbol of purity, and sacred fires are kept burning in fire temples (Agiaries). These unquenchable fires represent the awakened intellect and the light of God (Ahura Mazda). It would not be possible to perform any Zoroastrian rite or ritual without the presence of a sacred fire, or at least the representation of a sacred fire.

Purification

One of the essential practices of Zoroastrianism is that of purification. All people must keep their minds, bodies, and the environment pure to defeat the evil of Angra Mainyu and the Daevas. There are three types of purification that a person can undergo. In increasing order of importance, they are the padyab (ablution), then the nahn (bath), and finally the bareshnum.

During a padyab purification, the head and body are washed with water. This purification can be done by any person and does not require special blessings or a priest. First, a prayer is recited, then the hands, face, and feet are washed in that order, and then the hands are rewashed. This simple purification is done before and after engaging in any religious activity, such as praying or visiting a fire temple, or in any action that would render the person ritually unclean, including visiting a graveyard or using the restroom. Padyab may be performed at the beginning of each day's watch to acquire ritual power. The purpose of cleansing oneself is to wash away the evil of pollution symbolically.

For nahn purification, a ritual bath is taken. This will be done before a meaningful ceremony such as an initiation ceremony or a wedding and will also be done after childbirth. A priest is required to perform the nahn purification. First, the priest will recite a prayer and then give the person who is to be purified a pomegranate leaf to chew on, followed by a drink, to which a portion of the consecrated ash from the fire temple has been added. After this is done, the person and the priest will recite prayers of repentance, and then the person will bathe while the priest stands outside the bathroom door. When the bath is done, the person will say kusti prayers, clothe themselves, and rejoin the priest.

A bareshnum purification is intended for those entering the priesthood and takes 18-days to complete. The goal of this ritual is to purify and cleanse the body and the soul. For nine days, the initiate will sip a purification drink, exfoliate their body with sand, and cleanse themself with a bath in consecrated water. These first nine days are to cleanse themself. The following nine days are similar but done on behalf of the person in whose memory they are embarking upon the priesthood. Ritual prayers accompany each step of the purification.

Fire is the supreme symbol of purity within the Zoroastrian faith. Many cleansing and purification rites involve fire, either building a bonfire, leaping over fire, or otherwise involving fire. Fire symbolizes the spiritual flame, the source of wisdom, goodness, and vigor. Fire is also symbolic of the future when they would be cleansed of all evil by fire which the righteous will be able to pass through, but evil will not.

Sacred Chants

Zoroastrians believe that ritual chanting can bring about purity and order in the world as well as in the lives of believers. To please God and other spiritual creatures, manthras, or sacred passages from religious scriptures, are repeated in a particular manner. These poems are often written in Avestan, a Sanskrit sister tongue. Mantra recitation is supposed to be a practice of living by the three commandments, namely good words, good thoughts, and good deeds. The cadence at which the priest speaks the chants is also essential. The mantra consists of all these elements, and the chant is complete only when the words, intent, and cadence are correct. Many people use these chants repeatedly to fight against darkness on the inside and outside of the body. For those unfamiliar with Zoroastrian chants, there are many examples of the chants being spoken on the internet, which can familiarize people with the proper cadence to speak these chants.

One of the sacred chants is called Ahuna Vairya Mantra. It is said that Ahura Mazda spoke this mantra at the time of creation, and it helped him to manifest the whole of creation.

A Hama Zor Greeting, a ceremonial handclap, is typically conducted in a ceremony among the participating priests in addition to chanting and prayers. However, it used to be familiar to greet each other this way among the Parsis in India. For example, in a Jashan ritual, the head priest read blessing prayers. In contrast, the assistant priest would exchange handshakes with everyone in attendance, including clergy and laypeople, saying, "May you be of one power of one righteousness." This customary greeting helps the community members to stick together and advance justice.

<u>*Here is the procedure for the Hama Zor Greeting*</u>:

1. Standing side by side with their hands extended vertically, two participants face one another.

2. While simultaneously placing a right hand between each other's two hands and reciting the words "Hama Zor," all hands are joined and slowly slid out.

3. Reciting "Hama Asho Bade," they keep their eyes fixed on each other and simultaneously placed their left hands between each other's hands. They then connect all of their hands and slowly pull them apart.

"Hama Zor" means "Let us be united." "Hama Asho Bade" means "Let us be righteous." "Hama Zor, Hama Asho Bade" means "Let us be united in righteousness" when uttered collectively.

Sacrificial Rituals

Zoroastrians consider the conduct of sacrifice rituals, known as Yasnas, to be an essential aspect of their religious practice and the most effective way to interact with God and His beings. Moreover, an essential component of moral behavior is rituals. The rites are intended to purify both the participants in the world and the world itself. In a fire temple, they are often carried out by qualified priests while accompanied by Avestan chants. Zoroastrian scriptures strongly emphasize keeping ceremonial purity when executing the rituals to achieve the optimum results,

Additionally, five prayers are said five times a day by Zoroastrians. They perform an initiation process known as Naujote before initiating children, both girls, and boys, into the Zoroastrian faith. They also observe several well-known festivals to remember God and His entities.

Most ancient religions included a component of animal sacrifice. Common sacrifices are sheep and cows. The tradition suggests that sacrificing the animal will bring longevity and well-being to the owner of the animal or the community in general. Zoroastrians disagreed with this practice. There are a few places in the scripture where Zarathustra condemns this practice, talking about how Ahura Mazda disagrees with sacrificing animals. (Yasna 32.12, 32.14). Instead, Zarathustra teaches personal responsibility and that your misdeeds or sins cannot be transferred to an animal you then slaughter. Zoroastrians offer light, virtue, goodness, holy water, or wine to Ahura Mazda.

Sky Burials

Ahura Mazda and his soldiers do not enter Angra Mainyu's land of death. Angra Mainyu, therefore, rules the realm of death without any challenge. Angra Mainyu cannot touch the spirit since it is composed of the same substance as Ahura Mazda, and he is not strong enough to manage it. However, once the person dies, their spirit leaves their body, and from that moment, Angra Mainyu and the evil forces begin to take over the body. Zoroastrian literature gives remarkably detailed instructions on how to dispose of a deceased person's body. But, first, a body must be evacuated as quickly as possible, adhering to the guidelines established to safeguard those in the vicinity from the pollution caused by the evil presence of Nashu, an evil material.

The Zoroastrian writings advise putting a dead body on the flat top of a circular tower or a spherical structure called a dakhma that the priests created explicitly to dispose of bodies. The body would remain there until devoured by vultures, dogs, and other creatures that may prey on human flesh. The deceased's relatives should collect the bones once they are clean of flesh and dried in the sun. The bones are then placed in a vault, an above-ground ossuary, or a lime pit, where they should be left to degrade over an extended period slowly. The bones were permanently interred above the ground to prevent contamination of underground waters or the earth. The Zoroastrian religion forbids disposing of the deceased through burial, cremation, or throwing them into a river, lake, or ocean.

Zoroastrian priests and family members remember the deceased with rites and prayers and, as part of the funeral service, say special prayers to ensure the purity of the undertakers and the safety of the deceased's spirit. This procedure is the only way to dispose of a deceased person properly.

This practice may seem odd to many who are not part of the Zoroastrian religion, but Zoroastrians believe very strongly against the pollution of the earth and the water. Since the dead body begins to acquire and store evil forces as soon as the spirit leaves the person, causing the body's decay, they feel that these evil forces will taint the earth or water if the body is exposed to them. The belief is that the animals which eat dead flesh, such as vultures, were created by Ahura Mazda specifically to dispose of bodies.

In ancient Persia, sky burials were much more practical than any other method since the land was highly mountainous, and the ground was hard, rocky, and cold, making digging difficult. Additionally, fuel and timber were scarce, so cremation was not practical. However, sky burials were not unique to Zoroastrianism, and several ancient societies, including many Native American societies, may have practiced sky burials.

Sky burial is still practiced today in Tibet, Bhutan, and areas of Mongolia where certain Buddhist traditions are practiced. However, this practice has been outlawed in Iran since the 1970s. Many modern Zoroastrians in Iran tend to bury their dead in raised vaults, crypts, or mausoleums to prevent contact with the earth. For example, a former Qajar dynasty palace outside Tehran (Ghassr-e Firouzeh) has been purchased and turned into a Zoroastrian cemetery. The graves are lined with rocks and cement to prevent direct contact between the bodies and the earth. Some dakhmas remain in areas of India where the Parsi religion is practiced.

CHAPTER 2

SYMBOLS, SACRED SITES, SCRIPTURES, AND FESTIVALS

SYMBOLS

Religious symbols are recognizable images used to represent a particular religion or idea within a particular faith. Religious symbols can convey ideas about how people relate to the holy or sacred and the material and social environment. All religions use symbols to aid identification, signify membership in a specific group, or foster a sense of community among their followers.

Faravahar

The Faravahar is one of the most widely recognized symbols of Zoroastrianism. This symbol is seen etched into the stonework of temples and tombs, drawn on artwork and scrolls, and stamped into coins of the ancient Persian eras. The symbol depicts a bearded man wearing traditional Zoroastrian garb with one hand reaching forward and the other holding a circle. In the image, the figure stands over a set of wings extending from the middle circle, representing eternity.

There is no concrete evidence or universal agreement regarding its meaning, but many interpretations exist. It is commonly believed that it shows the fravashi or personal spirit. Other interpretations say that the man is Ashur, the Assyrian god of war, representing the never-ending war between good and evil. The feathered robe could also indicate a guardian angel, watching over all and aiding the people in fighting for good.

The Faravahar serves as a reminder to Zoroastrian people of their purpose in life:

> ➤ Stay away from negative influences.

> ➤ Strive for goodness.

> ➤ Behave well while on earth.

The three essential tenets of Zarathustra—good ideas, words, and deeds—are represented by the Faravahar. According to the most typical interpretations of the symbol, the human face stands for a link to humanity. The wings each have three rows of feathers. The upper row represents good reflections, the middle represents good words, and the bottom represents good deeds. The three rows on the tail, which are also present, stand for the negative thoughts, terrible acts, and wrong actions that, if not avoided, will result in human pain and disaster.

There are two loops on either side of the tail. One of them is directed forwards and represents Spenta Mainyu, the holy spirit, indicating that one should look toward the good in life. The other is directed towards the back and represents Angra Mainyu, the evil spirit, showing that one should turn away from the bad in life.

The circle surrounding the man's trunk represents how our spirit is limitless and has no beginning or finish. He demonstrates with one of his hands that people must struggle to succeed. But, on the other hand, the unbroken ring stands for fidelity and commitment.

The Faravahar is often seen as a fravashi or guardian angel but also represents divine grace, divinity, royal power, or personal spiritual power. It is representative of the tenets of Zoroastrianism.

Fire

Zoroastrian worship generally includes fire, and the temples are fire temples. In the past, Zoroastrians have been mistaken for fire worshipers. However, this faith is not about worshiping the fire but finding meaning and significance in the fire. The fire is considered the supreme symbol of purity, the light of God, and representative of the illuminated mind and warmth; it is the source of life. In some cases, people can experience godhood through fire and light.

In Zoroastrian fire temples, the sacred fires are continually fed so that it never goes out. In some of the oldest Zoroastrian fire temples, the sacred fire has been burning continuously for hundreds of years. Priests conduct prayers to the fires and tend them at least five times per day.

According to legend, Ahura Mazda himself built three fire temples in ancient Persia at the beginning of time when he created the world. These sites have been searched for by many over the years. Unfortunately, no locations have been verified, and whether they are genuine or legendary is unknown.

Fire is one of the main reasons the Muslims attacked the Zoroastrians when they conquered Persia. They compared Ahura Mazda with Satan since Satan is closely associated with fire. This contrasts with specific stories in the Quran, such as the one where God appears to Moses in a burning bush and other stories where God uses fire to send messages to his people.

The Number Five

The number five is sacred to Zoroastrians and will come up frequently, such as in the number of prayers the priests say to the sacred fire each day and the fact that festivals last for five days. The number five refers to the five celestial bodies that can be seen from the earth: the Sun, Moon, Mercury, Venus, and Mars. Zarathustra drew inspiration from the heavens, and stars and planets play a significant role in Zoroastrian beliefs.

The Avesta has a term for five called Pancha. Because it is associated with Sarosh Yazad, this number is primarily and most significantly significant in the Zoroastrian religion. Sarosh Yazad oversees compliance; hence he is responsible for the five senses and how they see the world, which determines whether a person is virtuous or sinful. The Gathas, the holy melodies of Zarathushtra, contain five documents: Ahunavad, Ushtavad, Spentomad, Vohu-khshathra, and Vahishtoisht.

The five gehs—Havan, Rapithwin, Uziran, Aiwisruthrem, and Ushahin—are the five divisions of the day according to Zoroastrianism.

There are five sections in society. These are:

- Nmana "home"
- Visa "village"
- Zantu "town"
- Dakhyu "country"
- Zarthushtrotem "global power."

The ten-day Muktad celebration is split into two intervals of five days each. The last five days, named after the five Gathas, are referred to as paj-i-meh, and the first five days, from roj ashtad to aneran, are the lesser five days, or panj-i-keh.

When performing most baj-dharna rites, the barsom ceremonial tool has five thin metallic wires. However, a five-twig barsom was employed even in antiquity.

The Yasnas list five virtues: righteousness, obedience, good thoughts, good words, and good acts. The five most grievous sins are wickedness, disobedience, bad words, terrible words, and evil deeds. Additionally, the priests divided themselves into five geographical regions in the 12th century for business purposes:

- Sanjana (from the Dantora River to the Par River)
- Bhagaria (from the Par River to the Tapi River)
- Godavra (from the Tapi River to the Narmada River)
- Bharucha (the Mahi River to the Narmada River)
- Khambata (from the river Mahi to the river Sabarmati).

The Number Seven

The number seven plays an essential role in the Zoroastrian faith as well. Ahura Mazda rules Heaven with his Heptad, the Divine Seven, which consists of Spenta Mainyu and the six Amesha Spentas. According to ancient writings, there are seven aspects to corporeal creation: fire, air, water, earth, plants, animals, and humans.

Zoroastrians believe in the seven acts of righteousness and aim to live in a way that embodies these:

- The generosity of the spirit
- Material generosity and sharing
- Honesty
- Community participation and inclusion
- Selfless help toward those in need (without desire for recognition or reward
- Piety
- Remembering one's ancestors

Seven is seen frequently within the Zoroastrian religion. Seven Ameshaspands, the highest divine beings in the Zoroastrian religion, look after the seven creations. The creator, Ahura Mazda, is an Ameshaspand and is seen as the father of the other six Ameshaspands. Their names are Dadar Hormazd, Shahrevar Ameshaspand, Bahman Ameshaspand, Ardibahesht Ameshaspand, Aspandad Ameshaspand, Khordad Ameshaspand, and Amardad Ameshaspand. This group is called the "haft Ameshaspand," or seven Ameshaspands, and the Haptan Yasht is dedicated to them. In addition, seven hymns are recited individually to invoke the Ameshaspands and Yazads.

Seven main virtues are associated with one of the seven Ameshaspands. These virtues are:

- ➤ Wisdom
- ➤ Peace
- ➤ Awareness
- ➤ Truth
- ➤ Perseverance
- ➤ Love
- ➤ Courage.

All other virtues stem from these essential virtues.

There are seven stages for the souls of the departed in the spiritual world. The three stages are Hell, which is referred to as Dushmata, Duzukhta, Duzvarshta, and the three stages of Heaven, which are referred to as Humata, Hukhta, Hvarshta. The middle stage, Hamestakan or Purgatory, is where souls go when the weight of their good deeds equals the weight of their evil deeds.

According to the Pahlavi book Denkard, seven nurses were present at the time of prophet Zarathushtra's birth. Some view these as an allegory for the presence of seven major celestial bodies at the time of prophet Zarathushtra's birth: the Sun, Mercury, Jupiter, the Moon, Venus, Saturn, and Mars, all of which were in good alignment.

The texts mention "hafta keshvar zamin," meaning the seven regions of the earth: Arezah, Fradadafsh, Savah, Vidadafsh, Khvaniras, Vouru Baresht, and Vouru Zaresht.

There is an Iranian tradition of setting the Haft-shin table just before the Jamshedi Navroz. In this table, seven (haft) articles starting from the letter shin (or even sin) are set on the table. The seven items usually include some of the following: Shir (milk), shakar (sugar), sharab (wine), shama (candle), somagh (sumac), sib (apple), shikeh (coin), sabzi (vegetables), shisheh (glass), sonbol (hyacinth), and sarkeh (vinegar).

When a Parsi couple marries, seven rounds of sutar (cotton) thread from a cotton ball (sutar no daro) is taken around the couple's chairs as they sit opposite each other.

The Cypress Tree

The cypress tree is a prevalent theme in Persian art and can often be found on Persian rugs. In addition, much Zoroastrian folk art features cypress trees representing eternity and long life. This is because cypress trees are evergreen and some of the longest-living trees in the world. They are fresh and green all year, easily withstanding the winter's cold and darkness, making them a perfect representation of everlasting life.

Priests or families would place branches from the tree around altars. This could be done for decoration, or the branches could be burnt on the fires during rituals. In addition, priests would plant cypress trees around temples to shade where the ancestor's bones lay.

Cutting down a cypress tree is a symbol of bad luck and would be seen as similar to destroying your fortune and allowing misfortune and illness to enter.

The Cypress of Kashmar

One specific tree told about for thousands of years is the Cypress of Kashmar. It is said that when Zarathustra visited Paradise, he brought back the branch of a cypress tree and then planted it in honor of his patron, King Vishtaspa's, conversion to Zoroastrianism. The tree grew in Kashmar, Iran. Stories say that it was located at the door to the fire temple at Kashmar, in the district of Turshiz. It was reported to be the giant, tallest, most expansive cypress tree ever recorded. It was said that many kings had recorded their acceptance of the Zoroastrian religion on its trunk.

On December 10, 861 CE, Abbasid Caliph al-Mutawakkil ordered his people to cut the tree down and transport it across Iran to Samarra. Since the tree was so large, and to discredit the Zoroastrian religion, he planned to use the wood as beams in his new palace. The Zoroastrian people protested the cutting down of the tree and raised a large amount of money to try to save it, but they were unsuccessful, and eventually, the caliph's men cut the tree down. The legend goes on to state that one day before the tree arrived at the palace, the caliph was killed by Turkish slaves. Some have suggested that his son employed the assassin, but this is unknown. The night the tree arrived at the banks of the Tigris, he was assassinated.

The scale of the tree was probably a myth, but the location, the fact that someone cut it down, and the caliph was assassinated were all established historical facts.

Paisley Design

Paisley, also known as "Boteh Jegheh," was developed during the Sassanid Empire as a unique pattern for usage in the Zoroastrian religion. The cypress tree, a symbol of eternity and life, is supposed to be represented by the curving curve of the paisley pattern, which is frequently compared to a teardrop or kidney shape with the upper end folded over. Mango, cashew nut, and sprouting date palm are some other examples of how to interpret the shape. However, there is significant debate as to whether the yin-yang symbol, utilized in traditional Chinese medicine and philosophy, was the source of this shape's original inspiration.

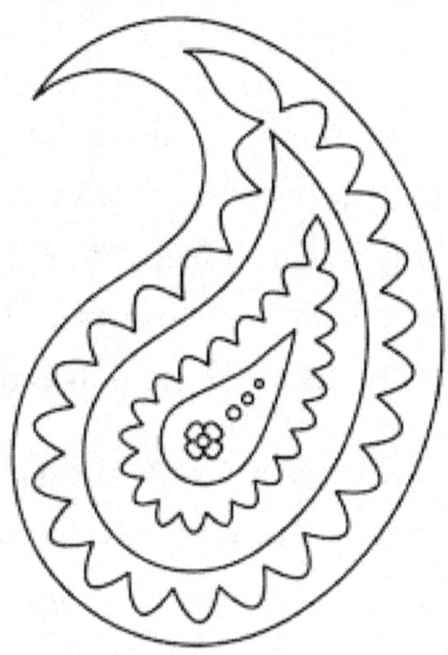

The paisley design is still very popular in modern Iran and India and can be found in clothing, artwork, and jewelry worldwide.

The Sudreh and Kusti

The sudreh and kusti are the garments that make up the traditional Zoroastrian religious outfit. The Sudreh is a long white shirt made of thin cotton fabric. Men typically wear a sudreh with a v-neck and a pocket over the chest. The pocket over the heart is symbolic of a place where the person could keep all their good deeds during the day.

Women usually wear a sleeveless version. The kusti is a long sash that is tied around the waist. It consists of 72 interwoven strands of wool, with each strand representing a chapter in the Yasna.

Together, the outfit symbolizes purity, light, and goodness. It is seen as the armor of God and is worn for all religious festivals and by priests to indicate that the person is pure and they are acting as a spiritual warrior for God. In addition, making garments out of cotton and wool reminds the wearers of the sacredness of plants and animals.

The Color White

In Persian literature and art, color has always played an important role. Color is also essential for religious orders, and often colors will identify how the community is supposed to feel about something. In addition, colors are often thought to have their spirits and to be able to enhance positive feelings or embody the attribute that is desired.

In Zoroastrianism, the priests wear white garments, and the sudreh and kusti worn by the public during festivals are also white. White is commonly linked with purity, peace, and cleanliness, representing that the people attending the ceremony or festival are entering the ceremonial space free from sin.

It is said that the people living in heaven or paradise will wear white silk and green silk. It is also often speculated that the faces of those who are blessed, the believers in the teachings of Zarathustra, will turn white on the day of doomsday, which is like the day of judgment in Christianity. In contrast, those who are not blessed will have their faces turn black. Being black-faced was associated with being dishonored. Throughout Persian history, people convicted of a crime had their faces blackened to make their crime and punishment visible to the community. A typical Persian expression "there is no color beyond black" means that there is nothing worse and relates to nonconformism and rebellion.

SACRED SITES

Dakhma / Tower of Silence

A dakhma, also known as a "Tower of Silence," is an elevated, circular enclosure built by Zoroastrians for excarnation or exposing dead people to the elements to rot. First, the flesh is eaten by carrion birds, most frequently vultures and other scavengers. Then, the skeletal remains are gathered in a central pit, where they continue to deteriorate and weather. The tradition in the Zoroastrian faith of exposing the dead to the elements may date to the middle of the 5th century BCE. However, contemporary documents begin recording this practice in the early 9th century CE. Sky burials and Towers of Silence prevent the dead bodies from coming into contact with the water or the soil. The natural environment is revered in the Zoroastrian religion and protected from the evil that comes with decay.

In the Iranian Zoroastrian tradition, the towers were constructed on hills or small mountains far from populated areas. In more populated areas in modern times, you may find the structures close to population centers, but this is simply because the cities have expanded since historical times. They are set apart from the city by gardens or forests. The structure or area will be composed of three concentric circles: the outer circle will contain men's bodies, the middle ring will be for women, and the center ring for children. Modern towers feature a nearly level roof, with the perimeter slightly taller than the center, and are constructed relatively uniformly. The ossuary pit will be at the center of the inner ring, where the bones are placed after cleaning them. In some areas, the bones will be treated with lime and washed with rainwater before passing through multiple coal and sand filters before draining into the sea.

In most cases, vultures can reduce the bodies to skeletal remains in about two hours, and in some cases, they can do it much more quickly. The bones are then swept into the center well after being dried by the sun. The ultimate act of kindness is to allow the carrion birds to eat the dead person's flesh since you give the animals food they need to survive.

The tower in Mumbai and the forest land surrounding it covers 54 acres of prime real estate near the city center. This tower uses solar panels to dehydrate the bodies, but many do not agree with this practice and would prefer to go back to a more traditional practice of using carrion birds. However, since the towers of silence have had large metropolises built up around them, there is a lot of concern about having birds eating human flesh and possibly dropping pieces of the flesh outside the tower area where it will be amongst the general population.

Due to various contributing factors, including the population of more and more land areas and a particular livestock drug that proved toxic to them, the population of vultures in India has decreased by 95% since the 1990s. As such, there are fewer birds available to perform the duty of disposing of the dead at towers of silence. The lack of birds meant that the undertakers were finding that bodies were not being taken care of as quickly as they should, which led to hygiene issues and resulted in installing solar panels as a solution. Most Parsis in the area would prefer that there was more focus placed on reinstituting the vulture population in the area. As a result, some scientific and government studies have been into vulture breeding programs over the years.

Agiary (Fire Temple)

An Agiary, literally the "home of fire," is a fire temple used by Zoroastrians during religious rites. There were roughly 160 fire temples located around as of 2021. Of these, about 45 could be found in Mumbai, 100 in other regions of India, and the remaining elsewhere. Nine fire temples are Atash Behram, the top tier of temples.

The idea of the eternal flame is thought to have originated from the practice of keeping the hearth fire burning throughout the life of the head of the household. This custom later evolved into the perpetual flame maintained in a place of worship as a tribute to and a representation of the Divine.

The deity of fire, Atar, was the fire itself yet transcended earthly fire as a divine creature created by the monarch of the gods, Ahura Mazda, and was revered in early Iranian religion. Atar and many other gods from the previous religion became extensions of Ahura Mazda once Zoroaster founded his monotheistic faith. The fire temples may have evolved from outdoor altars to enclosures during the Achaemenid Empire (550 – 330 BCE).

While the Greeks referred to the Zoroastrians as "fire-worshippers," they did not worship fire in these temples; instead, they worshipped the Divine, whose immanence was evident through the fire. Fire served as a metaphor for the divine element's energy, warmth, protection, and transformational qualities. The Parthian Empire (247 BCE - 224 CE) saw the establishment of fire temples, which peaked in sophistication during the Sassanian Empire (224 - 651 CE). Fire temples were demolished or transformed into mosques following the Sassanians' defeat by the Muslim Arab Invasion around 651 CE. However, it is believed that some of the flames from these temples were kept secretly burning by Zoroastrians and used to light the fires in succeeding temples. Most of the fires from this time were built by the Parsees of India. They later created fire temples and perpetuated Zoroastrian customs. These fires are still burning today in temples maintained by Zoroastrian populations in Iran, India, and other parts of the world.

When people enter the temple, they will offer some wood to the fire. The Vendidad and other places in the Avesta have listed the rules regarding what types of offerings are appropriate to make to the fire, which only allows wood as an offering. Most times, the offering will be sandalwood or some other type of wood that smells good when burnt. The offering is not added to the fire by the person entering the temple; instead, they will give the offering to a priest. The priest wears a mask over his mouth and nose during the procedure. The mask is worn to prevent any pollution from his breath from entering the hall of the fire. He will also use silver tongs to carry the wood to the fire so that no pollution from his hands touches wood.

The priest will use a spoon to scoop some ashes from the sacred fire after the wood has been added, and they will then be given to the individual who made the offering. This ash can be used on the forehead and eyelids as a blessing or in several rituals.

Different from many religions, most Zoroastrian priests do not preach or deliver sermons to the people. Instead, their role is to tend the fire at the temple. Each temple will have a chief priest, a dastur, who conducts worship ceremonies and blessings. There are three ranks of priests in the Zoroastrian temple. The lowest rank of a priest is that of herbad, who assists in the main ceremonies. The ordinary priests, mobad, tend to the fire and occasionally conduct worship services or perform marriages. The applicant must be a male descendant of a mobad, a son, grandson, or great-grandson, to qualify to train as a mobad. The dastur, who holds the highest rank and is in charge of all activities at the temple, undergoes a strenuous cleaning procedure to achieve this position.

Categories of Fires

The Behram, Adaran, and Dadgah are the three different types of fire. The categories indicate the level of respect and dignity in which these flames are held. Atash Behram, also known as the Fire of Victory, is the highest level of fire. This is the perpetual flame created in a Zoroastrian fire temple. Of all the fire categories, the development and consecration of the Atash Behram fire were the most meticulously planned. First, it involves collecting 16 different types of fire, such as lightning-caused flames (i.e., gathering up any tree branch that has caught fire), fire from cremation pyres, fire from jobs requiring furnaces, and fire from hearths, like in the case of the Atash Adaran. Following that, the 16 fires are ritually cleansed before coming together. The cleansing and consecration processes, which can take up to a year to complete, call for a sizable team of priests.

The goal of gathering and consecrating is to purify the fire to serve as a devotional object and an ever-pure symbol of Ahura Mazda that must never be put out. As an illustration, the revered Udvada Atash Behram at the Fire temple in Udvada was lit in Sanjan in 721 CE and is still burning today.

Atash Dadgah

The Atash Dadgah, the lowest category of the sacred fire, can be dedicated by two priests who alternately read the 72 lines of the Yasna rite for a few hours. The Vendidad can occasionally be pronounced during the consecration; however, it is not required. If no services are provided, a layperson may be able to handle the fire. Instead of merely a sacred fire, the word can also refer to an oil lamp or a fire in the hearth, typical in many Zoroastrian houses.

Atash Adaran

The Atash Adaran, often known as the "Fire of fires," is the fire with the next highest degree of intensity. It demands that representatives of the four professional categories, including the clergy, atheshtarih (soldiers and government employees), vastaryoshih (farmers and herdsmen), and hutokshih (tradespeople), assemble hearth fire. These four professional categories mirror feudal estates (artisans and laborers). Eight priests must dedicate an Adaran fire, which often takes two to three weeks.

Atash Behram

The Atash Behram is the most significant fire called the "Fire of Victory." Of the three, it has the strictest establishment and consecration rituals. First, it entails gathering fires from 16 distinct "kinds of fire," or sources, such as lightning, funeral pyres, work requiring the use of furnaces, and hearth fires, like in the case of the Atash Adaran. Following that, the 16 fires are ritually cleansed before coming together. Finally, the consecration process, which might take a year to complete, calls for 32 priests.

A temple must maintain not only an Adaran or Behram fire but also at least one Dadgah fire. Unlike the Adaran and Behram fires, the Dadgah fire is where priests carry out religious rites after which members of the public come and beg for blessings for a specific individual, a group of people, or an occasion. In Younger Avestan, larger fires are often revered by having the Atash Nyashes, a litany to the fire, recited in their presence. This is done so that only the fire itself is venerated with larger fires.

The 16 types of fire needed for an Atash Behram are:

- The fire used in burning a sacrifice
- Fire from an armorer
- Fire from a brewer
- The fire used by a dyer
- The fire from a king's house
- Fire from a shepherd
- Fire from a brick-maker
- Fire from an ascetic
- Fire from a goldsmith
- Fire from a mint
- Fire from a potter
- Fire from an ironsmith
- Fire from a baker
- Fire from a soldier
- The fire produced by lightning
- Fire from the house of a follower of Zarathustra

Fire rituals in the area of ancient Persia predated Zoroastrianism itself and were first noticed in the 9th century BCE. They were first recorded at about the same time as the shrine worship and generally coincided with Atar's debut as a deity. However, the Avesta does not refer to a temple of fire, nor does the Old Persian language include any words for such a structure.

The later Atash Nyash makes it clear that fire rituals were a doctrinal change and were not present in early Zoroastrianism. The hearth fire described in early texts speaks of the home cooking fire, which is inconsistent with sanctified fire. The temple was built much later; according to Herodotus, the Zoroastrians worshipped in the open sky in the middle of the fifth century BCE and climbed mounds to ignite their fires. Others who mention that the shrine at Zela in Cappadocia was a manufactured mound fenced in but exposed to the sky in the sixth century reaffirm this. Despite this, there is no proof that the Zela-sanctuary was Zoroastrian. Zoroastrian worship included fire burning, whereas many other religions also emphasized the presence of light and the eternal fire's burning.

In Zoroastrianism, there were two temples in the Parthian era (250 BCE – 226 CE). One was a sanctuary known as a bagin or ayazan, built in honor of the patron saint or guardian angel of a person or family and contained an icon or puppet of the adored deity. The "places of burning fire" that formed up the second category, the atroshan, multiplied as the movement gained popularity. After the Sassanid dynasty came to power, the Yazata shrines continued to exist, but by law, the statues had to be taken down or transformed into fire altars.

On Mount Khajeh in Sistan, close to Lake Hamun, the earliest known remnants of a fire temple exist. The ground plan and foundation are all that are still visible, and they have been provisionally dated to the third or fourth century BCE. Throughout the Sassanid dynasty (226 – 650 CE), the Parthians expanded and repaired the temple (250 BCE - 226 CE).

The dome-shaped sanctuary where the fire-altar was located was the Sassanid fire temple's distinguishing feature. A pillar in each corner of the sanctuary's square floor design always supported the dome (the gombad). In addition, the shrine may have had a corridor enclosing it on all four sides, according to literary evidence and archaeological artifacts. On many sites, all that is left are the gombads.

The Great Fires

Three fire temples are said to have been started by Ahura Mazda himself and therefore are the most important in Zoroastrianism. These "Great Fires" are located at Adur Burzen-Mihr, Adur Gushnasp, and Adur Farnbag. Stories from the third century CE indicate that these were also sites of miracles and are closely associated with the folk tales of Fereydun, Rustam, and Jamshid.

Although it is not known where these temples were, many archeologists have tried to identify their locations. Unfortunately, although there is reasonable certainty regarding where these temples may have been, this is still speculation.

Characteristics of a Fire Temple

A Zoroastrian fire temple's facade is typically straightforward and unadorned. This may be a relic from when people believed that a fire temple's principal purpose was to house a sacred fire rather than to be aesthetically pleasing.

Every contemporary fire temple shares the same basic design. Because there are no native records from before the 19th century mention an Iranian fire temple, so the existing temples in Iran probably have aspects that were original of Indian provenance. After entering, one goes into a big room or hall where special rituals or congregations might be held. The devotee then enters a smaller anteroom, potentially one story above or below the hall they just left, off to this side. The innermost sanctuary, which is connected to or housed within this anteroom but out of sight from the corridor, contains the actual atashgah or fire-altar.

A temple must always have a well, stream, or another source of natural water attached to it or on the grounds to perform a Yasna ceremony, which is the main Zoroastrian act of worship that goes along with the recital of the Yasna liturgy.

Only the innermost sanctum, which is enclosed on at least one side and has a double domed roof, is accessible to priests associated with a fire temple. Smoke vents are present in the double dome, but they are offset from one another to prevent rain or other material from getting into the inner sanctuary. The sanctum is elevated above the surrounding walls with huge gaps and divided from the anteroom by separators. Usually composed of marble or tile, the inner sanctum's walls are otherwise unadorned. The fire itself is the only source of illumination in the inner sanctuary. Temples are usually constructed to prevent direct sunlight from entering the sanctuary, a feature of Indian-Zoroastrian heritage that is not present in modern Iranian architecture.

A bell is hung in one corner as part of the boi ritual, and it is rung five times daily to mark the beginning of each gah, or "watch." It is always possible to obtain wood and other fire-starting items; you may typically find them hanging on the wall or, less frequently, kept in a small room accessible through the sanctuary.

Non-Zoroastrians cannot enter any location where they might see the fire. This is not required as part of the teachings in the Avesta, but it has become a custom.

SCRIPTURES

The Avesta

The Avesta is a compilation of essential texts which form the basis of the Zoroastrian teachings and religion. It comprises different texts written in an ancient Iranian language – Avestan. Some older texts are thought to have been written by Zarathushtra, but others have been added over time. The oldest documents have been dated back to the 2nd millennium BCE. The word Avesta means something similar to "praise," but the interpretation of the word is contested.

Initially, the rituals and prayers were passed on through oral tradition but later were written down. As the religion gained popularity and spread over the land, more rituals and prayers were added to the common practice, and the book was added. The first written Avesta was created when Zarathustra recited the prayers and hymns that he had received from Ahura Mazda in his vision. His patron, King Vishtaspa had these inscribed in the Avestan language to preserve them. Not many people would have been able to read at that time, as Avestan was primarily an oral language. During the Sassanian Empire, a script was created for this language based on Aramaic so that the scriptures could be recorded more permanently.

The Older Avesta refers to the oldest documents (Gathas, Yasna Haptanghaiti, and two prayers) written in the oldest language and the first sacred text. These texts are thought to have been present at the beginning of the religion and may even have been written by Zarathustra himself.

Younger Avesta is written in a more recent language and has had much more added to it as the religion has progressed. A widespread written Avesta was not thought to have been available until the late Sassanian Empire. Before that, much was shared through oral tradition. This later book contains myths, stories, and details of ritual observances.

The hymns of Zarathustra found in the Older Avesta cannot be definitively placed in their historical context because no places or people mentioned within them can be definitively dated. The only known facts are that Zarathustra lived in eastern Iran before Cyrius II the Great's unification of Iran. Moreover, the doctrine or preaching of Zarathustra is not mentioned in any modern literature.

Only the Gathas, the 17 hymns in the older Avestra, can be attributed to Zarathustra. They appear to have been created to preserve the prophet's teachings for subsequent generations soon after his passing. It is said that he either composed these hymns himself or received them directly from Ahura Mazda.

Gathas (the hymns)

These are the hymns or prayers recited by priests during ceremonies and rituals. These are not meant to be sung but are meant to be recited like poetry. These are the centerpiece and the most critical parts of inspiration in Zoroastrianism. Much of the writing includes wordplay and ambiguities, which initiates use as instruments to meditate and gain enlightenment. The Gathas are not written to instruct Zoroastrian followers but to invoke and glorify Ahura Mazda.

Many are written similarly to poetry and, when read in the original language, including clusters of lexical, semantic, and phonic language, which help promote a meditative state. For example, passages can be repeated like a mantra.

The teachings are unmistakable; they discuss the conflict between good and evil, the forces of truth (ashavans who worship Ahura Mazda) vs. lies (drugvants who worship the daevas), the goodness of Ahura Mazda, and the Asha and Vohu Mano. In addition, many teachings focus on the importance of offerings and rituals and the future rewards available for those who live a good life.

The 17 hymns are divided into six groups or chapters, which are usually named according to the first words of the first line:

- Ahunavaiti Gatha "Ahuna Vairya"
- Ushtavaiti Gatha "Having Happiness"
- Spenta Mainyu Gatha "Bounteous Spirit"
- Vohu Khshathra Gatha "Good Dominion"
- Vahishto Ishti Gatha "Best Beloved"
- Airyaman Ishya Gatha "The Invocation of the divinity Airyaman"

The Yasna Haptanghaiti

This is a group of seven hymns placed within the Older Avesta, and sometimes Zarathustra is also credited with writing it. Within the Yasna Haptanghaiti is where the Zoroastrian people were first introduced to the Immortals and told of some of their attributes and deeds:

- ➢ Praise to Ahura and the Immortals for the practice and diffusion of the faith.
- ➢ To Ahura and the Fire.
- ➢ To Ahura, the holy Creation, the Fravashis of the Just, and the Bounteous Immortals.
- ➢ To the earth and the sacred waters.
- ➢ To the soul of the kine.
- ➢ Prayers for helpers.
- ➢ Prayer to Ahura: The King, the Rewarder, the Life.

The Visperad

The book called The Visperad has 24 chapters. The word for "all the ratus" in the name is vispe ratawo. Its chapters were never meant to stand alone; they are recited along with many Yasnas. Additionally, it is not a component of Yasna's regular daily performance. Instead, its initial function was to adorn the Yasna ceremonial during the five major religious festivals. For example, prayers are recited while facing the sun, a fire, or a light source to invoke Ahura Mazda's divine force and light.

There are two separate meanings for the prefix ratu. "Season, a period," and hence "seasonal festival," are the simplest to define. The second meaning, which is more elusive, has generally been translated to signify "authority." The latter connotation of the phrase is frequently employed in the Visperad and is attributed to a wide range of deities, abstractions, and ordinary animals.

Only one line from the surviving Avesta bears the label "vispe ratawo," and that text is a later addition to the Younger Avesta. Stanzas 121–22 of Karda 30 are written in a Vendidad-style question-and-answer style: "Zarathustra questioned... Ahura Mazda said..." This section contains materials related to Mithra worship. The specific question at hand is how a good man should consume the purified libations to appease Mithra. In retaliation, they are told to take a ceremonial bath and endure whippings as a kind of penance. "Let no one drink of these libations who is not versed in the Staota Yesnya, the Vispe Ratawo," is the stanza's final commandment. Unfortunately, the relative phrase is grammatically erroneous; thus, it looks that vispe ratawo is an interpolation marking one of the two sentences that the worshipper is required to repeat. In any event, it is indicated that the worshipper must be able to recite the Staota Yesnya in addition to the Visperad because it is never performed by itself in documented Zoroastrian practice.

The chapters of the Yasna with the chapters of the Visperad inserted are included in the following chapter index.

- ➢ Yasna 1, verses 1 through 8, followed by Visperad 1
- ➢ Yasna 1, verse 10 through Yasna 2, verse 8, followed by Visperad 2
- ➢ Yasna 2, verse 10 through Yasna 11, verse 8, followed by Visperad 3.1-5
- ➢ Yasna 11, verse 9 through Yasna 15, followed by Visperad 3.6-7 through 4.2
- ➢ Yasna 11, verse 16 through Yasna 14, verse 5, followed by Visperad 5
- ➢ Yasna 15, followed by Visperad 6

- Yasna 16 and 17, followed by Visperad 7 and 8
- Yasna 18 through Yasna 21, verse 5, followed by Visperad 9
- Yasna 22, followed by Visperad 10 and 11
- Yasna 23 through Yasna 27, followed by Visperad 12 and then Vendidad 1 through 4
- Yasna 28 through 30, followed by Visperad 13 and then Vendidad 5 and 6
- Yasna 31 through 34, followed by Visperad 14, Vendidad 7 and 8, and then Visperad 15
- Yasna 35 through Yasna 42, followed by Visperad 16 and 17, and then Vendidad 9 and 10
- Yasna 43 through 46, followed by Visperad 18, then Vendidad 11 and 12
- Yasna 47 through 50, followed by Visperad 19, then Vendidad 13 and 14
- Yasna 51, followed by Visperad 20, then Vendidad 15 and 16, Visperad 21 and 22, and then Vendidad 17 and 18
- Yasna 52 and 53, followed by Visperad 23, and then Vendidad 19 and 20
- Yasna 54, followed by Visperad 24, and Vendidad 21 and 22
- Yasna 55 through 65, followed by Visperad 8, and then Yasna 66 through 72

The Vendidad

This is the Zoroastrian law book. Within the Vendidad are two sections speaking of how the law was given to humans, along with fragments of discussions held between Ahura Mazda and Zarathustra. Following this, there are 18 sections of rules regarding social behavior, moral laws, and specifying punishments for violations. This section is known as the "Law Rejecting the Daevas" because of its focus on laws and upholding morality. It contains a listing of all of the manifestations of evil spirits and ways to defeat them.

The Vendidad primarily focuses on preventing contamination in the physical sphere and is an essential source for our understanding of Zoroastrian purity standards. Chapter 9 of the Zoroastrian law book, for example, describes the nine-night purification ritual (barashnum nuh shab) for someone who has been tainted by touching a dead body.

Priests conduct the rituals listed in this section in the fire temple; some have parts for the priest to read and parts for the community members to read.

The Yashts

The Yashts are a group of 21 hymns of praise which are each dedicated to a specific deity or divine concept.

TITLE	IN PRAISE OF
Ohrmazd Yasht	Ahura Mazda
Hapt Amahraspand Yasht	the Seven Amesha Spentas
Ardawahisht Yasht	Asha Vahishta of "Best Truth"
Hordad Yasht	Haurvatat of "Wholeness" and "Perfection"
Aban Yasht	Aredvi Sura Ahahita of the waters
Hwarshed Yasht	Hvare-khshaeta of the "Radiant Sun"

TITLE	IN PRAISE OF
Mah Yasht	Manonghah of the "Moon"
Tishtar Yasht	Tishtrya, the star Sirius
Drvasp Yasht	Drvaspa, guardian of horses
Mihr Yasht	Mithra of "Covenant"
Srosh Yasht	Sraosha of "Obedience"
Rashn Yasht	Rashnu of "Justice"
Fravardin Yasht	the Fravashis
Warharan Yasht	Verethragna, "Smiter of resistance"
Ram Yasht	the "good" Vayu
Den Yasht	Chista, "Wisdom"
Art Yasht	Ashi of "Recompense"
Ashtad Yasht	Khvarenah, the "divine glory"
Zam Yasht	Zam, the "Earth"
Hom Yasht	Haoma
Vanant Yasht	Vanant, the star Vega

Ahura Mazda demands that these gods and divine ideas be praised, and the hymn is chanted both to invoke these beings or ideas for particular purposes and on the day of the month that day is dedicated to them. For example, Ahahita is noted to help women going through labor, so prayer to her (Aban Yasht) would be said when a woman is in childbirth to help ease her through. Likewise, Mithra presides over contracts, so the hymn Mihr Yasht would be said before entering a contract.

The Siroza

The 30 gods and divine ideas that rule over each day of the month are listed in the Siroza. In addition, there is a shorter Siroza, or "little Siroza," which lists their names and significant attributes, or a "great Siroza," which has more detail regarding each deity or concept. These are rarely read out in their entirety but used during the daily prayers in which the deity of the day is recognized.

The Nyayeshes

The five Nyayeshes are prayers that the community or priests can recite. For example, the Nyayeshes to the Sun and Mithra are recited together three times a day, the Nyayeshe to the Moon is recited three times a month, and poems to the Waters and Fire.

The Gahs

Each day watch or period is invoked by one of the five Gahs. Preachers in temples recite one prayer, or gah, for each hour of the day. Rapithwan is devoted to Ardibahesht and Ameshaspand, whereas Havan is dedicated to Meher Yazad. The Fravashis are honored at Uziran, Berez Yazad is honored at Aiwisruthrem, and Sarosh Yazad is honored at Ushahen.

Each gah has an invocation, an opening exhortation, a praise section, a conclusion, and finally, a closing blessing.

The Afrinagans

These are four texts that are recited when needed. One is recited to commemorate the deceased, another is unique to the five extra days after the Zoroastrian calendar year, a fourth is recited during each of the six seasonal feasts, and the fifth and last one is recited at the start and end of the summer. The five Gahs invoke the divinities who preside over each period or watch during the day.

FESTIVALS AND HOLY DAYS

There are many holy days in the Zoroastrian calendar, except for the Gahanbars and Nowruz, observance of the celebration is optional. Most celebrations, except those mentioned above, are done quietly either at home or at the temple, with the more significant celebrations involving community-wide festivities.

Gahanbars

The Gahanbars are six seasonal festivals that are celebrated throughout the year. It is a sin not to celebrate these festivals in the Zoroastrian tradition. These are significant community events that are acts of worship, and there is always a religious ceremony as part of the celebration. Each Gahanbar is traditionally five days, but community celebrations are often held on the last day. There are two segments of each Gahanbar, a religious ceremony followed by communal food sharing.

Gahanbars (also spelled Gahambar, Gahambar, or Gaahanbaar) are the only festivals mentioned in the Avesta and possibly instituted by Zarathustra himself. Although they are not mentioned by name in the Avesta, the Avesta does talk about six festivals in connection with the word yairya, meaning solar year. Therefore, the word Gahanbar could come from the Persian gah-ambar, meaning time gathering.

- ➢ Maidyozarem Gahanbar (midgreening), was observed from April 30 to May 4 in the middle of spring.

- ➢ A Midsummer festival known as Maidyoshahem Gahanbar is observed between June 29 and July 3. It is customarily observed on the summer solstice.

- ➢ The harvest celebration, known as Paitishahem Gahanbar (carrying in the corn), is observed from September 12 to September 16.

- ➢ Ayathrem Gahanbar (bringing home the cattle) - observed from October 12 to 16 to mark the end of the fall season.

- ➢ Maidyarem Gahanbar (mid-year) - A celebration of the winter solstice that lasts from December 31 to January 4.

- ➢ There is a festival called Frawardigan, also known as Hamaspathmaidyem Gahanbar, that takes place towards the conclusion of the year. This is traditionally observed from March 16 to March 20 and includes the spring equinox.

These festivals or high feast days are times when Zoroastrians assemble to eat and share food communally to celebrate an aspect of agricultural production. These celebrations are intended to demonstrate the Zoroastrian faith's beliefs, principles, and values. Everyone meets together regardless of status, with the rich and the poor all contributing to the feast, preparing and sharing the food equally. Contributing to the feast is an expression of egalitarian communal togetherness, and the food is contributed anonymously according to the person or the family's means and shared out equally. This helps to foster an environment of togetherness, goodwill, and sharing while building and strengthening the community. At the end of the feast, each person is gifted with a small bag of dried fruits and nuts to take home.

In Iran, a seventh Gahanbar is also celebrated, Tuji Gahanbar, instituted after the second world war when strict rationing was imposed. Those who had access to higher quality food shared their food with those who had none, and it was decided that after the war, this tradition would continue so that they could celebrate the spirit of sharing. This one is observed on the Vahram day of Aspandmard month (March 5 in the Gregorian calendar), and food is donated by the community and then distributed evenly.

Foods eaten at Gahanbar feasts can vary depending on the region and the season. Still, they will typically include some favorites such as Papeta ma gosht (meat in potatoes), Aush (a soup with fried bread), and always will include the Ajil or Lork/Lorg, which is a small packet of dried fruits and nuts that are distributed at the end of the feast.

A typical Ajil packet will consist of a mixture of seven types of fruit or nuts since seven is a sacred number. The contents of the mixture will be according to availability, but standard inclusions are:

- Almonds
- Apricots
- Cashews
- Dried mulberries
- Figs
- Hazelnuts

- ➢ Pistachios
- ➢ Raisins
- ➢ Roasted chickpeas
- ➢ Roasted squash or melon seeds
- ➢ Walnuts

Ajil is sometimes called ajil-e moshkel-gosha (problem-solving nuts) or ajil-e moshkel-asan (problem-easing nuts). According to tradition, a wish or problem will be resolved if we make a wish before consuming the bag's contents.

Maidyozarem Gahanbar

The first of the six great seasonal feasts, Maidyozarem is related to Shahrewar, a mystical figure who reigns over metals and minerals and is linked to the beginning of the sky. The dedicated equipment utilized to keep the sacred fire burning in Zoroastrian temples serves as a symbol for the celebration.

The gahambars were joyful celebrations that provided farmworkers with a much-needed reprieve from their labor, and they traditionally lasted five days. The first four days are devoted to getting ready for the feast on the fifth day.

Maidyozarem celebrations happen around these dates:

- ➢ Fasli – April 30 – May 4
- ➢ Qadimi – September 14 - 18
- ➢ Shenshai – October 9 - 13

Maidyoshahem Gahanbar

Maidyoshahem happens in mid-summer and is associated with waters. The festival is associated with Hordad, the Holy Immortal, and Amesha Spenta, who created water, and is the protector of wholeness and health. It appears that Maidyoshahem originated as a prehistoric midsummer event. It is a five-day festival from 11 to 15 Tir in the Zoroastrian calendar. The third day of Maidyosahem, Jashan-e Tiragan (13 Tir), is the most significant of the five days of Maidyosahem. Although Jasham-e Tiragan is a different feast, it has evolved into Maidyoshahem's main celebration. The Jashan-e Tiragan celebration connects nicely with Hordad because it honors Tishtar, the yazad of the star Sirius, and the pre-harvest showers.

Currently, Maidyoshahem is held on:

- ➢ Fasli – June 29 – July 3
- ➢ Qadimi – November 4 - 8
- ➢ Shenshai – December 4 – 8

Paitishahem Gahanbar

The third gahanbar of the year honors the arrival of the harvest and is connected to the formation of the earth. The five-day gahanbars, traditionally happy celebrations, gave the entire community a chance to come together and divide the labor necessary to complete the season's tasks. The first four days were devoted to feast preparation. Men, women, and kids in good physical condition labored in the fields to finish the seasonal tasks. Priests performed prayers while honoring worthy ancestors and asking for the village's and everyone else's well-being throughout the seven parts of the planet.

The fifth day was a feasting day. An ancient Avesta commandment, now known as Afringan e Gahanbar (or gahambar blessing), commanded all participants to bring a contribution of whatever they could afford to add to the standard pot — meat, vegetables, and grains. Additionally, people could provide firewood. Individuals who could not afford to make any form of contribution to contribute their time and labor.

The multi-ingredient stew, which served as a precursor to the Parsi staple dhansak and the Iranian dish aush, was then served as part of a community meal.

Paitishahem is celebrated on:

- ➢ Fasli – September 12 - 16
- ➢ Qadimi – February 16 - 19
- ➢ Shenshai – March 16 - 19

Ayathrem Gahanbar

Ayathrem has a meaning that is not apparent. It is believed to correspond to a time of abundance and sustenance, which explains why it is also known as the cattle breeding season.

Ayathrem celebrations currently are held around:

- ➢ Fasli – October 12 - 16
- ➢ Qadimi – March 14 - 18
- ➢ Shenshai – April 15 - 19

Maidyarem Gahanbar

Tradition dictates that Maidyarem be observed during a period in the agricultural year when all activity was suspended because of the harsh cold. The term airya, which means "rest," is where the name originates. In terms of theology, Maidyarem is linked to Vahman, the Amesha Spenta (or Holy Immortal) who made the original bull and all other livestock, as well as to virtuous deeds and intents. The Zoroastrian calendar's tenth month, Dey, observes Maidyarem from the sixteenth (Mihr) to the twentieth (Bahram) day.

Maityarem is currently held on:

- ➢ Fasli – December 31 – January 4
- ➢ Qadimi – May 2 – 6
- ➢ Shenshai – June 1 - 5

Hamaspathmaidyem Gahanbar / Frawardigan

Frawardigan is ten days where the souls of the dead are remembered. The last five days of the last month of the Zoroastrian calendar, as well as the five days that fall between the conclusion of the current year and the start of the next, are when this festival is observed. Muktad, a Sanskrit term that means "liberated soul," is the Parsi name for the Frawardigan days. The festivals of Pateti, Frawardigan, and Nowruz all happen simultaneously at the end/beginning of the year. Over time, these festivals have changed from separate events into multi-day events, incorporating them together.

Before the 1970s, Muktad in India was an 18-day festival that spanned the first seven days of Farvardin, the first month of the new year, from day Hormuzd to day Amordad, as well as the five Gatha days and the last six days of Asfandarmad, the month's final stretch from day Ashishvangh to day Aneran. In the 1970s, a group of high priests changed the Muktad to fit the standard 10-day Frawardigan, which included the last five days of the month before in addition to the five intercalary days. Because the switch to a 10-day Muktad was not widely embraced, each town may have a different festival.

In the month leading up to Nowruz, the house is traditionally thoroughly cleaned so that the cleaning is completed before Muktad. A marble-topped table is prepared in the house or temple and covered with a white cloth. A metal vase (karasya) with the name(s) of the person(s) who passed away in the previous year and is being remembered is placed on the table. Plates of prepared food and fruit are also set on the table. Prayers will be said every day, and the names of those who have been remembered will be read out. To invoke the fravashis, or guardian angels, prayers are recited over the foods, fruit, and flowers. Following the prayers, the participants will share the fruit and snacks. These rites might be carried out either in a temple or private by a family at their house.

A ceremony is held the final day to give the fravashis farewell.

This celebration happens on:

- ➢ Fasli – March 16 - 20
- ➢ Qadimi – July 12 - 16
- ➢ Shenshai – August 11 - 15

Name-Day Feasts (Jashan)

Throughout the year, there are 15 name-day feasts celebrated. During these feast days, all work stops except for necessary things, and the people make every effort to have a clean house and their best clothes for the festival day. After attending the religious services and saying prayers, all partake in sharing food and drink. Sometimes one individual would provide the food and drink for a feast, and others would contribute something to the feast. Some festivals had specific foods or other items associated with them, but all feasts would have wine, with many toasts, music, and dancing. It was common to find people telling stories, performing plays, or having chariot races or athletic contests. Some of these festivals may have developed out of regional celebrations.

Every feast is observed on the day that the names of the day and the month are the same. Four Jashans are observed in Ahura Mazda's honor during the tenth month since he is honored on four days each month. The first, eighth, fifteenth, and twenty-third days of this month are the Jashan of Dadvah and the Creator Feasts meant to honor Ahura Mazda.

The Amesha Spentas receive six Jashans during the year:

- ➢ On the second day of the eleventh month, the festival of Jashan of Bahman celebrates the creation of animals (January 16)

- ➢ Jashan of Ardavisht, which honors fire and other luminaries, is observed on the third day of the second month (April 22)

- ➢ Shahrevar's Jashan, observed on the fourth day of the sixth month, honors metals and minerals (August 21)

- ➢ The fifth day of the twelfth month is the date of Spendarmad's Jashan, which praises the soil (February 18)

- ➢ Jashan of (K)Hordad, which praises the water, is observed on the sixth day of the third month (May 25)

- Amurdad and Jashan observe a plant formation celebration on the seventh day of the fifth month (July 25)

The remaining five Jashans are dedicated to other yazatas:

- Farvardin's Jashan - held on the 19th day of the first month to commemorate the Fravashis (April 8)
- On the thirteenth day of the fourth month, Tir (Tiregan) celebrates Tishtrya and the showers (July 1)
- On the ninth day of the eighth month, Aban (Abanegan) honors Aredvi Sura Anahita and Apas, the waters (October 26)
- On the tenth day of the ninth month, Adaregans celebrate Atar and fire during Jashan of Adar (November 24)
- The 16th day of the seventh month is Mithra's festival, Jashan of Mihr (Mehregan) (October 2)

Other Holy Days

Pateti

Pateti is a day of penitence, repentance, and confession. The Persian word patet, which means regret, is where the word pateti originates.

The day after Pateti is Nowroz, which can occur at various periods throughout the year depending on which calendar is used. The Shenshai calendar, which the Parsis typically use, sets the new year in August in the present-day Gregorian calendar. This won't always be the case because leap days are not taken into consideration by the Shenshai calendar, which is why the day has gradually shifted from March to August. Nowroz is celebrated one month sooner by Zoroastrians who use the Kadmi calendar than those who use the Shenshai calendar. It coincides with the spring equinox for those who use the Fasli (seasonal) calendar (March 21). Currently, according to the Gregorian calendar, Pateti occurs in August.

Regardless of the day, it is celebrated, the customs of Nowruz and Pateti are very similar, with slight cultural differences. While the Fasli/Iranian Nowruz festivities are centered on Iranian Zoroastrianism, the Pateti customs are based on Indian Parsi Zoroastrianism.

People are urged to review their previous year's thoughts, words, and deeds on the day of Pateti and repent of any negative. When one repents, they have the opportunity to get forgiveness and have their soul cleansed, allowing them to concentrate on doing good deeds in the upcoming year.

On Pateti, the house's front entrance is embellished with chalk drawings, frequently featuring a fish with a red eye. Strings of flowers, usually tuberose or marigold, are strung over the tops of the doorways. Sandalwood incense is used throughout the home.

Before visiting the temple on Pateti, it is customary to bathe and then dress in new clothes. Because of this, people are often gifted new clothes for Pateti.

Food has a significant role in traditions. On this day, ravo, a breakfast dish prepared from sugi (semolina), milk, and sugar, is the custom. Also included is sev. Sev is fried vermicelli flavored with raisins and almonds and boiled in sugar syrup. For lunch and dinner, dishes like patrani-machchi, sali boti, moong dal, and pulao dal are regularly served. In addition, Suterfeni and galebi are popular candies on this day.

Making philanthropic contributions, dousing guests with rosewater as they enter a residence, and viewing comedic plays depicting the lives of the Parsis are other traditions associated with this event.

Sadeh

Sadeh is a mid-winter festival held 40 days after the winter solstice since it is said that the 40th night of the winter is the coldest. Therefore, it is also sometimes called Adar-Jashan. The celebrations begin on January 24th and end on February 3rd, ten days later.

During the festival, the people gather near a stream an hour before sunset and build a bonfire. The bonfire is always built near water since it is considered good luck to see the reflection of the fire in the water. Every community member brings some wood to contribute to the bonfire, as this is an actual community event. Before the fire is lit, there is a blessing ceremony for the community to support them through the remaining days of winter and the year to come. The light and heat of the bonfire symbolically drive back the cold and dark of the winter.

During the ceremony, the priest recites the "Ode to Fire" from the Avestan, and then the people will drink red wine, eat sugar-coated almonds and other nuts, and share heavy winter soups and other foods.

At the end of the festival, the embers from the fire are taken to the fire temple's sacred flame and each family's hearth so that they will merge with the eternal flame and with each family's hearth.

Historians note that the word Sadeh appears to be derived from the Persian numeral sad, meaning 100, but that doesn't have anything to do with the festival's timing. It is also possible that Sadeh may come from the Avestan word sareta, meaning means cold or freezing.

Ancient Iranian myths place the discovery of fire during the time of Sadeh, which started the age of industry and knowledge. In these myths, the fire was discovered by the epic hero Hushang. Seeking shelter on a cold winter night, he wandered into a mountain cave and saw a snake. He picked up a rock to strike the snake, but the rock was pyrite, and when he missed the snake and struck the cave wall, it created fire.

Hushang is credited with introducing the arts of metallurgy, building and construction, and the science of cultivating the soil and growing crops for the people.

Zartosht No-Diso

The eleventh day of the tenth month is marked as the anniversary of Zarathushtra's demise. Christians assemble for specific ceremonies in the fire temple on this solemn day, which include prayers, discussions, and arguments regarding the prophet's life and accomplishments.

Khordad Sal

This commemorates Zarathushtra's birth, and is first month's sixth day is when it is observed. His birth year is unknown, though it is accepted that he was likely born sometime at the beginning of the first millennium BCE. Khordad Sal is a celebration that brings together friends and family. Celebrants decorate their homes with flowers and rangoli, patterns produced with colored powder, for the floors or entrances. Zoroastrians visit friends, eat a feast, and make future resolutions after praying in the Fire Temple.

Hiromba

The people go into the wilderness to collect dry bushes and firewood. At sunset, the bonfire is lit. Priests give a blessing for health, strength, and prosperity for the living. The departed souls of each family are named and honored. After the bonfire, embers of the fire are mixed with the eternal flame and each family hearth.

Tirgan

On July 4, the Festival of Rain takes place. Legend says this is done to celebrate the end of an 8-year-long drought. On the day of the festival, it is customary for individuals to throw the rainbow-colored ribbons they have been wearing around their wrists for the previous ten days into a nearby creek and celebrate with sholeh zard, spinach soup, singing, dancing, and poetry recitation (saffron-flavored rice pudding).

Mehregan

Mehr, the goddess of light, friendship, love, and goodness, is remembered during the Persian fall festival known as Mehregan. In addition to celebrating the fall harvest, the event serves as a reminder of Zoroastrianism's virtues, virtues, and virtues. The tenth day of Mehr, often in October, is when it happens.

On occasion, believers set up a table with the Khordeh Avesta, a sormeh dan, and a mirror. The table also has incense, rosewater, candies, nuts, flowers, and fruits and vegetables. During lunch, the family offers prayers in front of the mirror. After eating sherbet, everyone applies kohl around their eyes as a good luck charm. Then, over each other's heads, they fling seeds and herbs. In the evening, participants worship light bonfires and fireworks and eat.

CHAPTER 3

AHURA MAZDA AND OTHER DEITIES

Zoroastrianism is a monotheistic faith, so there is only one God recognized by those that follow this religion. His name is Ahura Mazda, although he is known in other areas as Ahuramazda, Harzoo, Hormazd, Hurmuz, or Ohrmazd, which all mean "lord" or "spirit." Alongside Ahura Mazda and his Spenta Mainyu, or Holy Spirit, stand the Avesta Spentas, a set of six eternal beings that symbolize the attributes of Ahura Mazda that individuals are encouraged to aspire to in their life. Angra Mainyu and the Daevas oppose Ahura Mazda, which spreads evil throughout the world and tries to draw humans away from Ahura Mazda.

AHURA MAZDA

According to Zoroastrian traditions, the universe and everything in it were created by Ahura Mazda. He is the wise one and the ultimate example for all that is good. Ahura Mazda possesses many attributes, like other supreme deities. He is the uncreated spirit and the highest being in Garothman (heaven). There is nothing outside of him, apart from him, or without him. He has no equivalent, is unchangeable, moves without being pushed by anybody else, and no one can take the skies away from him. He upholds the truth and proper conduct, favoring the just man. Angra Mainyu, the destructive spirit, and Spenta Meynu, the benevolent spirit, are twin spirits that Ahura Mazda created, the former to spread destruction, deceit, darkness, and death, while the latter spreads light, truth, and life. The foundation of the Zoroastrian faith is the struggle between these two forces and the choice between good and evil faced by humanity.

The name Mazda may come from the Sanskrit word medhas, which means intelligence or wisdom, which fits with the description of Ahura Mazda as "Wise Lord." He is also called Ahuramazda during the Achaemenid era and is sometimes called Ohrmazd Ormazd.

According to legend, Angra Spenta became envious after Ahura Mazda created light. As a result, whenever Ahura Mazda produced something, Angra Spenta infused it with a small amount of evil. Sometimes, serpents are used to represent the two deities.

According to certain myths, the fight between Ahura Mazda and Angra Spenta, in which Ahura Mazda is the white monarch and Angra Spenta is the black one, served as the inspiration for the game of chess. The sixty-four squares on the board that are alternately black and white represent the floor of the House of Mysteries, while the chessmen represent the components of life. The chessman interacts with the components in the following ways:

- ➤ King – Immortal soul
- ➤ Queen – Mind
- ➤ Bishop – Emotions
- ➤ Knight – Vitality
- ➤ Castle – Physical body
- ➤ Pawn – Sensory impulses

Yes, the Japanese car company was named after the god Ahura Mazda. Since Azhura was the "God of Light", it was hoped that he would help to brighten the image of the car company.

SPENTA MAINYU (HOLY SPIRIT)

Ahura Mazda fashioned Spenta Mainyu to combat Angra Mainyu, the destructive spirit. Ahura Mazda can produce righteousness and life through him because he is a part of God. The sky, water, soil, plants, and unborn offspring are just a few of the various domains and species that Spenta Mainyu is said to guard and sustain. While humans frequently communicate with Spenta Mainyu, who subsequently serves as a conduit to Ahura Mazda, similar to other monotheistic religions like Christianity, Spenta Mainyu is not revered in his own right. Spenta Mainyu roughly means "Beneficent Spirit" in the Avestan language.

Spenta Mainyu is the oldest member of the great heptad of good spirits. The Amesha Spentas, or "benevolent immortals," help and serve Ahura Mazda by embodying good things about the world and running it following His ideals as opposed to Angra Mainyu and his evil counterparts, daevas or "demons." Angra Mainyu, Spenta Mainyu, and Ahura Mazda could be viewed as the spirits of the Netherworld Heaven, respectively. The heavenly spheres below are illuminated by the spirit above spirits within Endless Light.

AMESHA SPENTAS

The Amesha Spentas are six divine beings who are the highest beings after Ahura Mazda and are often seen as his holy counsel. The name Amesha Spenta means literally "bounteous immortal," and they are worthy of worship, although they are not worshiped directly, but as extensions or attributes of Ahura Mazda. Most frequently, they serve as a means for communicating with Ahura Mazda. Although the presence of a group of divine immortals suggests polytheism, they are not considered to be gods as Ahura Mazda is, but personifications of the abstract qualities that Ahura Mazda embodies. They can also be seen as archangels and ministers of the power of Ahura Mazda against the evil of Angra Maidyu. They are typically shown surrounding Ahura Mazda on golden thrones, surrounded by angelic beings. Each of them is honored with a month, a festival, and a flower, and a particular archfiend in later Zoroastrianism opposes each.

The Gathas, the primary sacred writings of Zoroastrianism, do not collectively provide any information about the Amesha Spentas. However, some are individually mentioned by name and feature importantly in some areas. For example, the word 'spenta' is found within these texts about the process of strengthening or increasing holiness. Within the Gathas, however, are a group of entities surrounding Ahura Mazda, and at times he is called the father of these beings. Many of the attributes that Ahura Mazda holds within the scriptures, such as Truth, Righteousness, and the Good Mind, become distinct beings and part of the Amesha Spentas as the religion progresses. It is noteworthy that many of the Amesha Spentas are quite like Vedic deities, and there is some speculation that these beings may have been brought in from previous religions to ease the way for the followers of Zoroastrianism as they transitioned from a polytheistic faith to a monotheistic faith.

In later texts, there is a heptad or group of seven entities related to Ahura Mazda that support him and do his work as required. These seven entities are the Amesha Spentas and Spenta Mainyu. While some hold that the existence of Spenta Mainyu and the Amesha Spentas represent a system of polytheism, Zoroastrians do not see it this way, as Ahura Mazda is the one true God. The Holy Trinity of the Christian faith, where God is the highest entity but also connected to and supported by the Son and the Holy Spirit, is a better comparison.

The six Amesha Spentas are the divine sparks of Ahura Mazda, and it was with their help that he was able to complete creation. Although Ahura Mazda is credited with creating the universe with his thought in various places in the Gathas, such as Yasna 31.11, it is more frequently believed that he sired six characteristics. This can be seen in passages such as Yasna 45.4. The influence of polytheism on Zoroastrianism may have contributed to making the Amesha Spentas more individual and giving them more form. Zarathustra's original teachings prescribed strict monotheism and did not allow worship of any being other than Ahura Mazda.

Ultimately, even though the immortal beings are considered divine, they are subordinate to Ahura Mazda and part of his creation. Each of the immortal creatures embodies a quality of Ahura Mazda's personality and makes it evident in the material world as a result of Ahura Mazda's divine will. Each person aspires to have and develop the qualities represented by the Amesha Spentas to nurture Asha and become an ashavan (possessor of truth).

Asha Vahishta and Vohu Manah are the two of the six that are most important. The way things occur in the universe is according to the natural order of the cosmos, or Asha Vahishta. He is in charge of the fire, which Zoroastrians treasure as a symbol of reality as it truly is. He presents the follower with the path of righteousness and divine knowledge. Vohu Manah is the name of the spirit of divine knowledge, illumination, and love. He brought Zoroaster's soul before the throne of heaven. In heaven, Christ extends a cordial greeting to the blessed souls. Believers are encouraged to "bring down Vohu Manah in your life on Earth" through true love in marriage and for one's neighbor.

Each of the Amesha Spentas has evolved distinctive traits over time, and they are each connected to a particular physical element and domain. They are frequently portrayed as the physical element with which they are related. Along with Ahura Mazda and Spenta Mainyu, each of the Amesha Spentas has a day during the first week of the month. Members of the Amesha Spentas are frequently depicted as humans wearing traditional cloaks and caps, along with the element with which they are linked. Vohu Manah, Asha Vahista, and Kshathra Vairya are either male or non-gendered, while Spenta Armaiti, Haurvatat, and Ameretat are depicted as feminine.

Ameretat (Immortality)

Ameretat is the personification of immortality. She plays a crucial role in creating the Haoma, a drink that is said to temporarily confer immortality to anybody who consumes it, as she is the embodiment of long life leading to immortality. She represents a long life that leads to immortality. The responsibility for safeguarding the plants necessary for life's survival falls to Ameretat (or Amurdad). Since Haurvatat and Ameretat have complementary healing and life-giving properties, they are commonly mixed. Zarathustra refers to them together as the nourishment of Ahura Mazda. These two Amesha Spentas also represent the spiritual entities that are most distant from Ahura Mazda. They are only entirely recognized after death and the ensuing judgment; thus, this is not a sign of their inadequacy. Instead, it reflects their role during the last phase of a soul's existence.

Asha Vahista (Truth)

Asha Vahista (or Ardavisht) is the Amesha Spenta that is most frequently mentioned in the Gathas, albeit Zarathustra might have been referring to Asha Vahista as an example of a principle rather than the entity itself. Followers of Zoroastrianism strive to become ashavans and live by Asha, the cosmic principle of truth and order. Asha Vahista represents Asha. Asha Vahista is therefore closely associated with truth and righteousness. Asha is said to be the heavenly quality that most effectively counteracts the demonic spirits' tactic of druj, or lying. Commonly, Asha Vahista is associated with luminaries, especially fire. For instance, in the Yasna, he is manifested by fire, demonstrating his enormous significance because fire is the focal point of the Yasna ritual and is regarded by Zoroastrians as the most significant of the physical elements.

Haurvatat (Wholeness and Health)

Haurvatat, also known as Hordad, represents abundance and perfection. She oversees the water, demonstrating her vital role in preserving a healthy lifestyle. In the Yasna ritual, water is her symbolic representation. Consecrated water, pomegranates, goat milk, and twigs are combined with consecrated water at one stage in this ritual. Then, to provide its strengthening properties to all creation, this combination is thrown into a particular well outside the pawi. As a result, the ritual makes use of water to tap into Haurvatat's integrity and wholeness because she can so quickly affect all of creation.

Khshatra Vairya (Good Dominion)

The Good Dominion of Ahura Mazda is represented by Kshathra Vairya (also known as Shahrevar), who personifies the principles of rightful kingship and social order. The ashavan is reminded of the value of authority in the temporal domain by Kshathra Vairya. Every level of society, from the head of the family to the king or queen, must have this authority. Kshathra is not connected to any aspect of creation in the Gathas; it is only in later literature that he is referred to as the protector of metals and the sky. By reviewing the evolution of cosmogony over the epochs, contemporary scholars explain this unusual marriage of sky and metal. In Stone Age cosmology, the sky—which is thought to be made of stone—is mentioned as the first of the creations, but metal is not one of them. This is also reflected in Zarathustra's epiphany when he claims that the sky is "of the hardest stone" (Yasna 30.5). Kshathra thus became linked to stone. The belief is that the sky is made of crystal; therefore, both stone and metal later developed after the development of bronze and iron instruments (Yasht 13.2). Kshathra's association with a solid stone firmament gradually gave way to one with a metallic sky. He eventually developed a connection to metals in general. The metal instruments that the officiating priest and his aide use are a representation of Kshathra Vairya in the Yasna, which demonstrates this.

Spenta Armaiti (Devotion)

The element of Ahura Mazda that stands for commitment and piety is called Spenta Armaiti (or Spendarmad). Because she is responsible for preserving the planet, Zoroastrians have a solid connection to the creation she stands for. Because of Spenta Armaiti's connection with the planet, she is often represented by the consecrated ground of the ritual area, or the pawi, in the Yasna rite. She is praised for keeping watch during the Yasna ceremony over the pawi and the surrounding area. Because of her omnipresence, she overcomes the bounds created by the division between the sacred area and the outside world, symbolizing the relationship between consecrated and unconsecrated objects.

Vohu Mana (Good Mind)

As evidence of the value that both entities place on one another, Vohu Mana (or Vahman), which is Sanskrit for "Good Mind" or "Vision," is cited in the Gathas almost as frequently as Asha Vahishta. The two appear to form some Gathic triad with Ahura Mazda. Vohu Mana represents the discernment and clarity of awareness that Ahura Mazda bestows on those who adhere to his truth. Zarathustra and other Zoroastrian adherents can recognize Ahura Mazda's holiness thanks to Vohu Manah. Ahura Mazda bestows his wisdom through Vohu Mana by either choosing to bestow knowledge or abilities upon a person or by amplifying the wisdom or virtue that a person has previously attained through their efforts. All of the animals created in the physical world connect to Vohu Mana, notably cattle, for which he serves as the protector. Vohu Mana was once represented in the Yasna by a sacrificed animal. Even though live animals are no longer used in this ceremony nowadays, Vohu Mana is symbolized by dairy products like milk and butter and a sieve made from a consecrated bull's hair. The sieve separates herbs and solid particles from milk during rituals or sieves ashes from the sacred fire.

Zoroastrian texts state that time is both endless and finite and that space is both visible (getig) and invisible (menog). Beyond the reach of the senses, the invisible world is nevertheless accessible through the inner spirit and inner eye. The six Amesha Spenta archetypes and the angels serve as its representation and inhabitants.

The seven creations: sky, water, earth, plant, animal, human, and fire, live in the visible universe and are represented by material objects formed of the four elements: fire, water, air, and earth.

Some Zoroastrian texts claim that Ahura Mazda is made up of both the visible and invisible realms. Angira Mainyu, the evil spirit, did not want an order to rule when God manifested the visible universe. He so succeeded in getting past the objects made of metal and tried to wreak havoc. Because of this, pollution was able to get into the ground, air, and water, killing, rotting and destroying humans, animals, and plants.

However, as fire is a kind of light, it cannot be contaminated or penetrated by evil, and therefore, it will always be revered.

Zruvan akarana, or infinite time, is indivisible, unalterable, unbreakable, and eternal. It has no length, beginning, or end because it is absolute. In contrast, a finite time is prone to destruction and change. It is both cyclical and linear. The past and future are separated from linear time. The cyclical time is divided into four periods, each lasting 3000 years.

God ensured that evil stayed limited to its area and remained finite throughout limitless time. He enticed the evil entity to enter both of them when He made the finite time in the visible world so that he would eventually be confined and destroyed. Thus, according to Zoroastrianism, time and space are seen as snares or traps made by God to draw in and contain evil spirits so that they might be destroyed. The following verse demonstrates how God is credited in Zoroastrian texts with having the ability to move objects in space.

Be aware that the power of the unseen spirit is used to make people want to move. No one can move about or perform labor in this world without a spirit or soul. The existence of the spiritual essence that causes life and motion in the material body is what sustains the force of motion in the living body that moves and functions (in this world).

ANGRA MAINYU (EVIL SPIRIT)

The evil, destructive spirit in the dualistic cosmology of Zoroastrianism is called Angra Mainyu, also known as the Destructive Spirit or Ahriman in Middle Persian. He is said to be Spenta Mainyu, the Holy Spirit's twin brother. Both were sons of Ahura Mazda, the Wise Lord and principal deity of Zoroastrianism, according to the earliest version of the story.

Gluttony, rage, and envy are Angra Mainyu's three central vices. Angra Mainyu attacked Ahura Mazda's good creation Spenta Mainyu, enlisting the aid of a swarm of jealous and like-minded demons in the process. Despite the havoc and suffering that Angra Mainyu's onslaught has caused, believers are confident that Ahura Mazda will ultimately triumph. His demons will devour one another within their dominion, ending his existence. In a later version of dualism, Ahura Mazda is still the creator god, and Angra Mainyu is his wicked, destructive opposite. Both are forever present.

The modern Zoroastrians of India, the Parsis, tend to minimize the importance of Angra Mainyu by explaining it away as a metaphor for humanity's worst tendencies. Ahura Mazda reclaims his omnipotence as a result.

Daevas

A daeva is a hostile supernatural creature, according to Zoroastrianism. The daevas are described as "gods that are to be rejected" in the earliest scriptures of the Zoroastrian canon, the Gathas. The Old Persian "daiva inscription" from the fifth century BCE contains a similar interpretation. The daevas are said to be divinities that promote uncertainty and disarray in the Younger Avesta. The divs are portrayed as personifications of every sort of evil in subsequent tradition and folklore. Later, Islam adopted the story of Daeva as Div.

The root of the word "Deva" in Hinduism and the Iranian language are the same. The terms for Vedic spirits and Zoroastrian entities have different functions and develop conceptually, although sharing a standard derivation. The phrase was first applied to mythical beings that were present before the scripture was written. There is not much written about the Daevas individually in the Avesta, and much of the information comes from legends or stories passed down through generations.

Aeshma

The demon of wrath in Zoroastrianism is known by the name Aeshma. He is associated with wrath, anger, and fury and often goes by the name "of the bloodied mace." Aeshma inspires violence and destruction and is usually depicted carrying a bloody spear. He is the opposite of the Amesha Spenta Ahsa Vahishta, or truth, and Sraosha, Obedience. He acts as the messenger of Angra Mainyu. Aeshma's primary goal is to distract people from proper worship and lead them towards violence and drunkenness.

Aka Manah

The Gathas, the earliest Zoroastrian books thought to have been written by Zoroaster himself, mention the idea of Aka Manah. Aka Manah is a demonic being and a supporter of Angra Mainyu in the Younger Avesta.

Angra Mainyu created Aka Manah as the evil mind to counteract the excellent mind of Vohu Manah. In the scene of the prophet's temptation, Aka Manah joins the plan of the demon Buiti to attack Zarathushtra. He practices his cunning by using deceptive words of seduction to urge the sainted leader to stray from the path of righteousness, but the holy prophet resists the devil's plan. Additionally, this evil being futile, takes part in the conflict between the forces of the Good Spirit and the Evil Spirit for the Divine Glory. Therefore, Vohu Manah will defeat Aka Manah at the end of the current cycle. Consequently, according to Zoroastrianism, the power of Aka Manah will ultimately be destroyed by Vohu Manah since good will triumph over evil on the Day of Judgment.

Apaosha

Aposha is the name of the demon of drought in Zoroastrianism. He is the opposite and antagonist to Tishtrya's, the goddess of rain. Apaosha is often referred to as Aposh or Apaush in Zoroastrian scriptures.

For many years, it was believed that the Avestan word for drought, apaosha, came from either apausa, which means burning away, or apavta, which means stemming the waters. Today, scholars speculate that it simply means "not flourishing."

In the narrative recorded in Yasht 8.21–29, Tishtrya rides a mighty white horse with golden ears and a tail as he sprints toward the celestial sea Vourukhasha. Apaosha, a hideous black horse with black ears and a black tail, greets him there. After three days and nights of fighting, Apaosha expels Tishtrya. Then, Tishtrya bemoans to Ahura Mazda that he became weak since no one made the required prayers and offerings for him. When Tishtrya returns to the fight with Apaosha at midday and eventually conquers the demon of drought, Ahura Mazda presents a sacrifice to her. After that, everything returns to normal as Tishtrya permits the rain to fall freely on the soil.

According to specific interpretations, this story combines an astronomical and seasonal event: Tishtrya's star Sirius rises heliacally in July, right before the year's warmest and driest period. Sirius is a shining star that can be seen around dawn during the upcoming several days (doing battle with Apaosha). The star Sirius appears to brighten throughout the stifling summer months as it becomes more directly visible (Tishtrya gathering strength), eventually becoming steadily visible (Apaosha vanquished). The rainy season begins with Apaosha's defeat (in late autumn).

<u>Busyasta</u>

The Zoroastrian daeva of sloth is called Bushyasta. "The long-handed" is often used to describe her. She is described in the Vendidad and Yashts as gaunt and having a color of yellow or green. Bushyasta is not among the demons who are described in great depth, even though she is one of the few daevas who are particularly referenced in the texts.

Bushyasta is the hypostasis of idleness and laziness in scripture as well as later tradition. She tries to prevent the virtuous (Ashavan) from completing worthwhile activities; hence she is the source of procrastination. She soothes everyone back to sleep and causes the pious to forget the prayer hour while they are dozing off.

Indra

Indra is an ancient Vedic deity in Hinduism and the King of the Daevas in Zoroastrianism. He is linked to the sky, lightning, thunder, weather, rain, storms, river flows, and battle. The tales and abilities of Indra are reminiscent of those of other Proto-Indo-European gods, including Zeus, Jupiter, Perun, Perknas, Zalmoxis, Taranis, and Thor. Indra is amoral and quick to temper, reigning by strength and acting according to his own will. He is the leader of the Daevas and second after Angra Mainyu.

He is often shown riding on a white elephant and carrying his weapon shaped like a lightning bolt.

Jahi

The demon of lewdness in Zoroastrianism is known as Jahi. In his role as a hypostatic being, Jahi has been described as a hussy, rake, libertine, harlot, or someone who lives a passionate or sometimes debauched life. She is often referred to as "the Whore." In addition, Jahi is depicted as Ahriman's consort and the origin of the menstrual cycle in Zoroastrian mythology.

When the contaminated whore sits down and consumes the offering Haoma intended for her, the devotee in the ode to Haoma resists her allure. In the song to Asha, the holy phrase manthra spenta serves as a potent barrier against Jahi and other deadly beasts. In the ode to Ashi, "Fortune" bemoans how ashamed she is of Jahi's unethical actions.

It also briefly alludes to Jahi's cosmological function as the assassin of Gav-aevo data, the initial animal that gave rise to every subsequent animal development. Jahi is the one who causes Ahura Mazda "the most sorrow," according to Vendidad.

Tradition holds that near the close of the second cosmic age (the second 3000 years), Jahi's cunning schemes provoked Ahriman to awaken from his impotence and vow to exterminate the people of Ohrmazd. Ahriman had so far resisted his demons' pleas up until that time. Ahriman defiles her with a kiss after being provoked, and as a result, Jahi is now having her period. Ahriman designates Jahi to pollute females, and this defiling results in menstruation in females. Jahi is reported to have a glance that may end lives.

Malkus

In Zoroastrianism, Malkus, "The Destroyer," is a Daeva who oversees the excessively long winters, keeping the people from being able to plant fields and encouraging starvation. He is a dangerous monster from Zoroastrian literature identified as having a destructive nature and a Turanian Bradarores ancestor who murdered Zarathustra.

Nasu

Her Avestan name, Nasu, knows the female Zoroastrian daeva of corpse matter. She lives in the northern region, the location of Zoroastrian hell. Nasu, who appears as a fly, represents the decomposition and pollution of corpses (nasa). When someone dies, Nasu takes up residence in the body and speeds up the decay process. Nasu appears in several Avesta writings, most notably the Vendidad, which strongly emphasizes demons, purifying rites, and the destruction of corpses and other dead stuff. Nasu is frequently regarded as the world of Ahura Mazda's greatest polluter. Nasu-belief has significantly impacted Zoroastrian funeral rites and burial procedures, as well as the culture's fundamental contempt for dead bodies.

Nasu and other female daevas are frequently preceded by the prefix "druj," which means "demoness." The feminine Avestan term for the lie, druj, means the opposite of asha, or truth. All entities who opt for druj over asha are referred to as possessing falsity by the adjective whose origin is druj. Various Avesta texts employ the word "druj" with diverse connotations. Druj may be used to allude to demons or as a catch-all term for everything wrong, immoral, or unclean, depending on the context.

Saurwa

Sauvra is the enemy of Khshathra Vairya, an angel. Unfortunately, the Avestan scriptures, which mention this demon's name, do not provide us with information about his life, although he is noted to oversee misrule among the people.

CHAPTER 4
HISTORY OF THE RELIGION

TIMELINE

TITLE	IN PRAISE OF
Approximately BCE 1500 – 1000	Scholarly estimates on the life of Zarathustra Zarathustra develops the tenants of Zoroastrianism
Approximately BCE 728 – 550	The Dynasty of the Medians
BCE 549 – 329	The Dynasty of the Achaemenids The Achaemenid Empire unofficially adopts Zoroastrianism
BCE 247 – CE 224	The Parthian Period, and the Dynasty of the Arsacids Zoroastrianism continued during this period
Approximately CE 224	Zoroastrianism becomes the official state religion in Persia
CE 224 – 651	The Dynasty of the Sassanids Zoroastrianism is endorsed by the Sassanian Empire
CE 309 – 379	Shapur II dedicated Zoroastrian literature to writing for the first time.
CE 531 – 579	The Sasanian Empire's Kosrau I's reign Zoroastrian religious writings are codified and written down.

TITLE	IN PRAISE OF
Between CE 633 - 651	Persia was conquered by Muslim Arabs. Zoroastrianism is suppressed and persecuted
CE 752 – 804	The Dynasty of the Abbasids
Approximately CE 785	Zoroastrians began to move to India to escape Persecution by Islam
CE 821 – 1055	The Iranian Intermezzo and the Persian Renaissance
CE 819 – 999	The Dynasty of the Samanids
CE 821 – 873	The Dynasty of the Tahirids
CE 861 – 1003	The Dynasty of the Saffarids
CE 889 – 929	The Dynasty of the Sajids
CE 919 – 1062	The Dynasty of the Sallarids
CE 931 – 1090	The Dynasty of the Ziyarids
CE 934 – 1062	The Dynasty of the Buyids
CE 1037 – 1153	The Dynasty of the Selijuks
CE 1256 – 1353	The Mongols and the Dynasty of the Il-Khanid
CE 1370 – 1508	The Timurid Empire and Ottoman Turks
CE 1500 – 1736	The Dynasty of the Safavids
CE 1722 – 1730	The Afghan Interlude
CE 1736 – 1747	The Reign of Nadir Shah
CE 1751 – 1779	The Dynasty of the Zands
CE 1789 – 1925	The Dynasty of Qajar
1851	First Parsi-Muslim Riots
1925 – 1979	The Dynasty of the Pahlavis
1979 – Present	The Islamic Republic of Iran

BEFORE ZOROASTRIANISM

The prophet Zarathustra, known as Zartosht in Persian and Zoroaster in Greek, is commonly thought to have lived between 1500 and 1000 BC. The antithesis of the Indo-Aryan religion that would later be known as Hinduism, ancient Persians acknowledged the gods of the old Indo-Aryan religion before Zarathustra. Zarathustra declared that the Lord of Wisdom, Ahura Mazda, is the only deity worthy of adoration and that he forbade this practice. The teachings of Zarathustra may have led to the development of the first monotheistic religion, and it may also have widened the gap between Iranian and Indian Aryans.

THE PERSIAN EMPIRE

The Zoroastrian religion significantly impacted the mighty Persian Empire, one of the most prominent historical empires. For three notable Persian dynasties, it was the official religion. Some researchers contend that the Persian Empire strongly affected Zoroastrianism, which impacted the three major Abrahamic religions—Christianity, Judaism, and Islam. In addition, the Silk Road, a network of trade routes connecting China with the Middle East and Europe, also helped Zoroastrianism spread throughout Asia.

Through nomadic tribes, Zoroastrian teachings started reaching people across Persia and neighboring areas. With the aid of the Magi, a priestly group with Medes roots, Cyrus, the Persian empire's first monarch, spread Zoroastrianism throughout Egypt, Greece, Persia, and parts of India. The three Magi, who came to Bethlehem to see Jesus when he was born, most likely belonged to the same priestly group. When Alexander overthrew the Persian Empire in 331 BC, Zoroastrianism briefly declined in Persia. But when the Sassanians defeated the Parthians and formed their dynasty in the third century AD, it once more came to life. The Sassanians adopted Zoroastrianism as their official religion. They granted the priests certain rights to spread their religion among the populace while acknowledging their religious authority as a significant component of their political power. Therefore, during their time, the state and the religion merged into one. This idea was comparable in many ways to the one used by the Romans when they adopted Christianity as the official religion. During this time, the Magi gave Zoroaster's teachings a strict interpretation and labeled any disagreement with them as heresy and treason.

THE MEDIAN DYNASTY (APPROXIMATELY BCE 678 – 549)

The Medes were a group of prehistoric Iranians who lived in the Media region between western and northern Iran and spoke Median. They established themselves in northeastern and eastern Mesopotamia, adjacent to Hamadan, as well as the hilly terrain of northwest Iran during the eleventh century BCE (Ecbatana). Around the eighth century BCE, they are thought to have met in Iran. It is unknown how much of the other areas the Medians controlled in the 7th century BCE, although they did dominate over all of western Iran.

The Medes have not left any written documents behind them, despite having a considerable impact on the history of the ancient Near East. As a substitute, one must rely on historical documents from other civilizations, including Assyria, Greece, Armenia, Babylon, and a few Iranian archaeological sites that may have been Medes-occupied. According to Herodotus, the Medes were influential individuals who established an empire at the beginning of the seventh century BCE that would have lasted until the middle of the fifth century BCE. The Medes significantly assisted in the fall of the Assyrian Empire and fought wars with Lydia and Babylonia. However, archaeologists did not discover the earliest Median sites in Iran until the 1960s. Before the 1960s, the main focus of the hunt for Median archaeological relics was the "Median triangle," which contains Hamadan, Malayer, and Kangavar, all in the province of Hamadan.

There is no distinction between "Persians" and "Medians" in Greek references to "Median" people; a Greek who immersed themselves too profoundly in Iranian culture became Medianized, not Persianized. An Iranian state known as the Median Kingdom had a brief history and scant literary and archaeological records. Despite this, it left a lasting and essential mark on Iranian civilization. Sadly, there aren't many materials that discuss the Median people's religion. Archaeological finds from Tepe Nush-e Jan, names from the Middle Ages, and Herodotus' History has been used as primary sources to demonstrate the Medes' religious ties. The ancient temple constructions in Iran reportedly contained a fire altar, suggesting the nation's long-standing association with a cult of fire.

According to Herodotus, the Median Magi were a tribe that supplied priests to both the Medes and the Persians. They had a caste of priests who were counselors, dream interpreters, and fortune tellers in Astyages' court. The priest's duties were passed down from father to son.

All early historians agreed that the Magi were priests of the Zoroastrian religion. There are instances of the Indo-Iranian word arta- (truth), which is recognizable from both Avestan and Old Persian, as well as theophoric names like Mazdakku and the name "Ahura Mazda" in the personal names of the Medes that the Assyrians recorded (in the 8th and 9th century BCE). Astyages and perhaps even Cyaxares, according to some researchers, had already embraced a religion based on Zoroaster's teachings. In contrast, others claim that the Magi's presence in Media and their rites and devotional practices prevented Zoroastrian proselytizing there. Scholars have differing opinions about the integrity of the Medes' Zoroastrianism proof. Additionally, there have been theories that Mithra is a Median name, the Medes were Mithraists, and Mithra was their most revered deity.

THE ACHAEMENID DYNASTY (APPROXIMATELY BCE 549 – 329)

After overthrowing the Medes dynasty in 549 BCE, Cyrus the Great led the Persians in the quick establishment of the first Persian empire and the second Iranian dynasty. The fire-altars discovered at Pasargadae and the fact that Cyrus gave his daughter the name Atossa—the name of the queen of Vishtaspa, the royal patron of Zarathustra—indicate that he may have been a Zoroastrian, though no inscriptions from his reign mention his religion. The majority of historians concur that Cyrus was a tolerant king who let his citizens who were not Iranian practice their religion. He governed according to the Zoroastrian principles of asha (truth and justice). Still, he took no steps to convert or repress the customs of the inhabitants of the nations that Persia had conquered.

The transmission of Zoroastrian ideas, including the concept of a single deity, heaven, hell, and a day of judgment, may have begun in the Jewish community in Babylonia, where people from the Kingdom of Judea had been prisoners for years. The Jews of Babylon were freed when Cyrus overthrew Babylon in 539 BCE. Many returned to Jerusalem, where their progeny contributed to the creation of the

Hebrew Bible, in which many of the ideas presented align with Zoroastrianism.

By Darius the Great, the empire was Zoroastrian (549 – 485 BCE). In one of his inscriptions, Darius mentioned Ahura Mazda, the powerful creator of the land, the sky, man, and happiness for man. The same inscriptions attest to Ahura Mazda's choice of Darius as the sole ruler over all other kings.

The magi were in charge of religion during the Achaemenian Dynasty (c. 549 - 329 BCE). Aristotle was one of many Greek historians who wrote on Zarathustra. They all referred to him as the "Master of the Magi" and described him as a Persian prophet. They were reported to follow unusual rituals involving the dead, dealing with evil animals, and interpreting dreams, all of which had hazy parallels to Zoroastrian practices. Zoroastrianism must have reached western Iran before Aristotle's time because he references the dualistic nature of this newly emerging religion in several of his writings (384 - 322 BCE).

THE PARTHIAN PERIOD (APPROXIMATELY BCE 247 – CE 224)

From 247 BCE until 224 CE, the Parthian Empire, often referred to as the Arsacid Empire, dominated Iranian politics and culture. The latter name derives from the tribe's founder, Arsaces I, who led the Parni tribe in the conquest of Parthia during an uprising against the Seleucid Empire. At the time, Parthia was a region in northern Iran controlled by Andragoras. Mithridates I conquered Media and Mesopotamia from the Seleucids, extending the realm (which reigned roughly 171 - 132 BCE). At its height, the Parthian Empire, which began on the northern Euphrates in central-eastern Turkey, covered what is now Afghanistan and western Pakistan. Additionally, the empire expanded as a hub of trade and commerce due to its location on the Silk Road trade route between the Roman Empire and the Han dynasty of China in the Mediterranean Basin.

The art, architecture, and religious customs of the Parthians' culturally diverse realm, which included Persian, Hellenistic, and indigenous cultures, were heavily influenced. The Arsacid court adopted aspects of Greek culture for roughly the first half of its existence before progressively reintroducing Iranian customs. The Arsacids, who followed the Achaemenid Empire, made various local kings their vassals in place of the Achaemenids' centrally chosen but mainly independent provinces. Even though the majority of the governors were located outside of Iran, the court did name a handful of them, but these provinces were not as strong as those ruled by the Achaemenid dynasties. As the Arsacid empire expanded, other cities assumed the role of capital, and Ctesiphon, south of modern-day Baghdad, Iraq, along the Tigris River, became the new administrative hub.

The Seleucids in the west and the Scythians in the north were the Parthians' first adversaries. However, as Parthia grew to the west, they clashed with the Armenian Kingdom and eventually the defunct Roman Republic. Rome and Parthia fought a battle to subjugate the rulers of Armenia. At the Battle of Carrhae in BCE 53, the Parthians decimated Marcus Licinius Crassus' army, and in BCE 40–39, they finally destroyed the Romans in the Levant, except for Tyre. Despite Mark Antony's propensity to win battles without taking part, his lieutenant Ventidius launched an attack on Parthia. Throughout the succeeding Roman-Parthian Wars, several Roman emperors or their selected generals attacked Mesopotamia throughout the following few centuries. Throughout these campaigns, the Romans frequently took Seleucia and Ctesiphon, but they were never able to maintain them. When Ardashir I, king of Istakhr in Persia, rose against the Arsacids and killed their last emperor, Artabanus IV, the Parthian era ended in 224 CE. The internal struggles of the Parthian king-seekers were a more significant threat to the security of the Empire than foreign invasion. As a result, the Sasanian Empire, established by Ardashir, ruled over much of the Near East and Iran until Muslim conquests in the seventh century CE. But the Arsacid dynasty endured because several family branches held power in Albania, Iberia, and Armenia's Caucasus.

Sasanian and even older Achaemenid manuscripts are more common than native Parthian texts written in Parthian, Greek, and other languages. As a result, Parthian history can only be studied using unofficial sources, including fragments of ostraca, rock carvings, drachmas, and the remarkable survival of some parchment documents. There are histories of China since the Han Chinese attempted to forge coalitions to fight the Xiongnu, but most are histories of Greece and Rome. Historians consider Parthian art to be a reliable source for understanding facts about society and culture that are not present in written sources.

Due to its diversity in culture and politics, the Parthian Empire had a broad spectrum of religious beliefs and ideas, with Greek and Iranian cults predominating. Except for a minimal number of Jews and early Christians, the bulk of Parthians were polytheists. Deities from Iran and Greece were frequently combined. Zeus, Aphrodite, Hermes, Hades, Apollo, and so forth were frequently compared with Ahura Mazda, while Anahita and Mithra were put in opposition to one another. Each ethnic group and city had its collection of deities in addition to the major gods. According to Parthian art, the Seleucid and

Arsacid rulers both regarded themselves as gods; this may have been the most common kind of monarchical religion.

Modern scholarship is divided on the importance of Zoroastrianism to the Arsacids. The horrific sacrifices made by numerous Iranian religions during the Parthian era would have repulsed Zoroastrians. However, there is proof that Vologases I invited Zoroastrian magi, priests, to the court and urged them to peruse the Avesta's library of Zoroastrian religious literature. Later, the Sasanian court would acknowledge Zoroastrianism as the imperial religion.

SASSANID DYNASTY (CE 224 – 651)

The Sassanid Dynasty (224 - 651 CE), which also encouraged Zoroastrianism's ascent, made it the official religion of the Persian Empire. Before the arrival of Christianity, Zoroastrianism was a widely practiced religion, and the Sassanids made an effort to spread it throughout the lands they governed for centuries, especially in modern-day Azerbaijan.

Because of its connections to the Christian Roman Empire, which had been Persia's principal enemy since Parthian times, the Sassanids were apprehensive of Christianity. After Constantine the Great's reign, Christians were occasionally persecuted. The Sassanid emperors' battle with their Armenian subjects at the Battle of Avarayr (451 CE) led to their formal separation from the Roman Church.

The Nestorian Church, which is said to have been founded by Thomas the Apostle during the first century CE as a gateway to bring Christianity to the East, was the only version of Christianity that the Sassanid Empire accepted and occasionally encouraged.

Although it was still commonly practiced as late as the 5th century CE as something close to a second recognized religion, Zoroastrianism gradually lost ground as Christianity spread.

MUSLIM CONQUEST (BETWEEN CE 633 – 651)

The Muslim conquest of Persia between 633 and 651 CE resulted in the fall of the Sassanian Persian Empire and the extinction of Zoroastrianism in Iran. The Arab invaders tormented the Zoroastrians living in Persia, enforced laws to make their lives harder, and levied additional taxes because they continued practicing their religion. In the end, the majority of Iranian Zoroastrians converted to Islam, which replaced them as the nation's official religion.

Under the first four Caliphs, Zoroastrianism remained the dominant religion in Persia. However, Zoroastrians now have the title of dhimmi, or People of the Book, thanks to Caliph Umar. Although they were treated as second-class citizens and many of their religious practices were outlawed, they were nonetheless allowed to retain most of their status.

Zoroastrians endured severe religious discrimination, persecution, harassment, and identification as impure to Muslims in the centuries that followed, deeming them unfit to coexist with Muslims, driving them from cities, and subjecting them to harsh punishment in all spheres of life. Zoroastrians endured prejudice in society, academia, and the job, as well as humiliation in public because of dress rules.

During the Islamic conquest of Persia in 637, the Zoroastrian palaces and their archives were destroyed. This led to the loss of the Persian capital of Ctesiphon in the Khvarvaran region, now known as Iraq. At the time, Sa'ad ibn Abi Waqqas was in charge of the soldiers.

Caliph Umar ibn al-Khattab stated that the texts were blasphemous if they conflicted with the Qur'an in response to the question of what should be done with Ctesiphon's books. But if they concur with the Qur'an, then the Qur'an suffices, and others are not required. There is debate over whether the enormous libraries were intentionally burned down or looted. Still, either way, the books—the work of Persian academics and scientists for centuries—were destroyed and dumped into the Euphrates.

A further 40,000 individuals were slain or hanged in the southern city of Estakhr, a Zoroastrian religious center, as they fought against the Arab invaders. In Arabia, over 40,000 Persian noblemen had been abducted and sold as enslaved people.

Under the late Umayyad Caliphs, whose dynastic ancestors had mostly subdued the final Zoroastrian empire by 652, persecution increased during the 8th century. The Caliphs imposed a jizya tax was imposed on Zoroastrians, and Arabic took the place of Persian as the official language. In 741, the Umayyads formally outlawed non-Muslims from holding positions of power.

To lead the expedition to the Mazandaran, a general of the Umayyads called Yazid-ibn-Mohalleb was granted leadership of a considerable force. However, to allow the Arab army to pass through on its advance toward victory, the general issued the order to hang prisoners on both sides of the road leading to Mazandaran.

The majority of the atrocities performed against the Zoroastrian populace during combat were committed by the Umayyads, who were ruthless in their pursuit of victory over their Zoroastrian adversaries. The Zoroastrians who submitted to their rule did get the safety and some level of religious tolerance, nevertheless. There are rumors that

Umar II told his followers not to destroy a church, synagogue, or a place of worship for people who worship fire (perhaps the Zoroastrians) if they had submitted to the Muslims. Zoroastrians in northern Iran suffered little, and in exchange for paying a tribute levy, or jizyah, they were granted almost total autonomy. At this period, there were still a significant number of Zoroastrians living in northern and western Iran.

THE DOWNFALL OF ZOROASTRIANISM

From Mesopotamia to the Indus River, Persia (modern-day Iran) was dominated by a Zoroastrian majority. Before the Arab invasion and subsequent Muslim subjugation, it was an independent political state. In 224 CE, Zoroastrianism was recognized as the official state religion during the Sassanian Empire, the last of the four pre-Islamic Persian empires. Zoroastrianism's dominance over Persia's religion was instantly weakened by the Arab conquest, which also rendered Islam the country's official religion.

ABBASID DYNASTY (CE 752 – 804)

With the assistance of Iranian Muslims, the Abbasid Dynasty overthrew the Umayyads. Temples and sacred-fire sanctuaries were demolished, Zoroastrian persecution intensified substantially, and Zoroastrian people received official recognition as a minority during the Abbasid dynasty. Because of the change in their position from "kafirs" to "zimmi," or non-believers, throughout the Abbasid dynasty, Zoroastrians were not accorded the same standing and privileges as Jews and Christians. Iranian Muslims were allowed admission into the court, but Zoroastrians were excluded. Zoroastrians were prohibited from using bathhouses because their bodies were considered dirty.

Zoroastrianism faced harsh opposition from the Abbasids due to their brutal treatment of non-believers and extensive funding of Persian Muslims. For example, abdollah-ibn-Tahir, an Arabicized Persian who served as the Abbasid caliphs' administrator of Khorasan, allegedly forbade Persian printing and ordered all Zoroastrians to bring the holy books they might be burned. As a result, numerous literary works written in Pahlavi were destroyed.

But there were plenty of instances of tolerance during the Abbasid era, particularly under the direction of Al-Mu'tasim, who openly mocked an imam and muezzin for tearing down a fire temple and erecting a mosque. Nevertheless, al-Mu'tasim permitted Zoroastrian fire temples to be reconstructed and rebuilt in several locations inside the bounds of the Abbasid Caliphate. According to reports, there were still sizable numbers of Zoroastrian strongholds operating under the Abbasid government in cities like Kerman, Qom, Sistan, Fars, and others. Their presence is confirmed by contemporary Muslim historians who were present and later European explorers.

THE IRANIAN INTERMEZZO/ PERSIAN RENAISSANCE (821 – 1055)

Following the Islamic invasion of Iran in the seventh century and the fall of the Sasanian Empire, a period known as the Iranian Intermezzo or Persian Renaissance developed. This period witnessed the development of numerous indigenous Iranian Muslim kingdoms in the Iranian Plateau. The term is significant because it served as a transitional period between the Arab decline of Abbasid dominance and power and the "Sunni Revival" that began with the rise of the Seljuq Turks in the 11th century. Iranian support based on Iranian land and, most significantly, a renewed Iranian national spirit and culture in an

Islamic form made up the Iranian renaissance. The Iranian Intermezzo comprises the Iranian dynasties and organizations known as the Tahirids, Saffarids, Sajids, Samanids, Ziyarids, Buyids, and Sallarids.

In actuality, the Iranian Intermezzo includes several Iranian, predominantly Kurdish, minor dynasties in the provinces of Armenia, Albania, and Azerbaijan.

The Dynasty of the Samanids (CE 819 – 999)

Aristocratic Zoroastrians known as the Samanids freely switched to Sunni Islam. Nearly 300 years after the Arab conquest, there were fire temples in almost every province of Persia under their rule, including Khorasan, Kirman, Sijistan, and other areas ruled by the Samanids. Even in Baghdad, according to folklore, there may have once been fire temples. Zoroastrianism continued to be practiced over time in various parts of Iran. Not only in countries that were provinces of early Muslims, like Tabaristan but also in those that came under Muslim domination much later. The fire temples in Iraq, Kirman, Fars, Tabaristan, Sistan, Khurasan, Azerbaijan, al Djibal, and Arran are revered by the Madjus, according to folklore.

The Samanids advanced science and literature by revitalizing Persian culture and fostering the arts, which attracted geniuses like Rudaki, Ferdowsi, and Avicenna. According to scholars, while revitalizing Persian more than the Buyids and Saffarids had, the Samanids nonetheless preferred Arabic for religious and academic study. They thought they had a connection to the Sasanian Empire.

Although the Samanids actively supported Sunni Islam and crushed Ismaili Shiism, they were more tolerant of Twelver Shiism. People in the Samanid dynasty started converting to Islam in substantial numbers once the first complete translation of the Qur'an into Persian was finished in the ninth century. Compared to the Tahirids, who were almost wholly Arabized, the Samanids were only marginally Arabized. Although Arabic science and literature flourished throughout the Samanid Empire, the Samanids were able to have a significant influence on the revival of the New Persian language and culture thanks to their independence from Baghdad. The earliest Islamic culture to adopt a language other than Arabic was of this Persianate type.

The economic pillars of the Samanid State were trade and agriculture. The Samanids traded extensively with Europe. In the Baltic and Scandinavia, many Samanid coins have been discovered.

The Dynasty of the Tahirids (CE 821 – 873)

A Sunni Muslim dynasty with Persian dehqan roots, the Tahirids ruled over Khorasan from 821 to 873 and oversaw Baghdad's military and police forces under the Abbasids until 891. The Tahirids established Merv as their first capital before relocating to Nishapur. The Tahirid Dynasty was a joint venture with the Abbasids rather than a separate dynasty. They enjoyed great liberty in exchange for their loyalty to the Abbasid caliphs. In essence, they served as viceroys for Abbasid power in Persia.

Ishaq, one of the governors of Baghdad at the time, oversaw the Mihna (inquisition), which targeted everyone who was not a follower of Sunni Islam and persecuted them. During his administration, the caliphs relocated to Samarra, a newly built city, replacing Baghdad as their capital. Two of Ishaq's sons ruled after him when he passed away in 849, and Muhammad ibn Abdallah, Tahir's grandson, took over in 851. The Mihna, one of the few instances of particular religious persecution in medieval Islam, lasted for 18 years before being discontinued.

The Dynasty of the Saffarids (CE 861 – 1003)

From 861 to 1003, the Saffarid dynasty, a Persianate monarchy with roots in eastern Iran, ruled over some of Greater Iran. One of the earliest indigenous Persian dynasties to emerge after the Islamic invasion was the Saffarid dynasty. Ya'qub bin Laith as-Saffar, the dynasty's founder, was an ayyar from Sistan who initially worked as a coppersmith (affar) before rising to power as a warlord. He began to encircle most of Iran after capturing Sistan, a sizable chunk of Afghanistan, and smaller portions of Pakistan, Tajikistan, and Uzbekistan.

The Saffarids started a bloody eastward and westward advance from their capital Zaranj. In 873, they made their first forays into the areas south of the Hindu Kush, overthrew the Tahirid kingdom, and seized power in Khorasan. Ya'qub had gained control over the Kabul Valley, Sindh, Tocharistan, Makran (Balochistan), Kerman, Fars, and Khorasan by the time that he died. He had also been on the point of arriving in Baghdad before the Abbasids forced him to turn around.

After Ya'qub's passing, the Saffarid dynasty did not last very long. Ismail Samani defeated Amr bin Laith, his brother, and his successor at the Battle of Balkh in 900. Amr bin Laith was forced to hand over the majority of his domain to the new overlords. The Saffarids were confined to the region of Sistan, which functioned as their homeland. Over time, and under the Samanids and their successors, their status deteriorated to that of vassals.

By encouraging Persianate culture and the Persian language through court poetry, the Saffarids took great care to maintain Persian culture. Persian poets who achieved fame in the eastern Islamic world during their rule included Abu Salik al-Jirjani, Fayrouz Mashriqi, and court poet Muhammad ibn Wasif. Zoroastrian institutions were frequently overthrown and taken over as Persian civilization developed. The Zoroastrian clergy fell out of favor as soon as it lost official funding.

The Dynasty of the Sajids (CE 889 – 929)

From 889 to 929, the Iranian Muslim Sajid dynasty ruled. First from Maragha and Barda, then from Ardabil, the Sajids dominated much of Azerbaijan and a tiny portion of Armenia. The Sajids were of Iranian (Sogdian) ancestry and came from the Ushrusana region of Central Asia. As the first Sajid monarch of Azerbaijan, Muhammad ibn Abi'l-Saj Diwdad succeeded his father Diwdad in 889. Abu'l-Saj Devdad, the father of Muhammad, later fought for the caliphs in Azerbaijan against the rebel Babak Khorramdin after helping Ushrusanan prince Afshin Khaydar in his final conflict there.

Muhammad was able to establish a primarily independent kingdom as the Abbasid Caliphate's centralized power started to wane around the end of the ninth century. The Sajids concentrated much of their efforts on attempting to subjugate the neighboring Armenian nation. In 914, Yusuf ibn Abi'l-Saj devised a plot to attack Georgia. Tbilisi served as the base of military operations. After capturing several territories, he initially took control of Kakheti and the castles of Ujarma and Bochorma.

With the passing of Abu'l-Musafir al-Fath in 929, the dynasty came to an end. The Sajid dynasty was overthrown in Ardabil by poisoning one of his enslaved people, which also made way for the Sallarid dynasty's eventual expansion into Azerbaijan in 941.

The Dynasty of the Sallarids (CE 919 – 1062)

In the second part of the tenth century, the Iranian Muslim Sallarid dynasty dominated the regions of Samiran, Tarom, Daylam, Gilan, and later also Arran, Azerbaijan, and some areas of Eastern Armenia.

Daylamites who seized control of Shamiran, a mountain stronghold 25 miles north of Zanjan, were the Sallarids' leaders. They established their dominance over the surrounding Tarom region from Shamiran and formed marriage relations with the Rudbar-based Justanid dynasty, which was a close neighbor.

Muhammad bin Musafir was the Sallarid in charge of Shamiran at the start of the 10th century. He became involved in the Justanids' internal conflicts after marrying one of them. But finally, even his own family turned against him as a result of his authoritarian rule, and in 941, his sons Wahsudan ibn Muhammad and Marzuban imprisoned him.

While Marzuban attacked Azerbaijan and overthrew its monarch Daisam, Wahsudan stayed in Shamiran. Marzuban defeated attacks from the Mosul Rus and Hamdanids, took control of Dvin, ended the Sajid dynasty in 941, and founded the Sallarid dynasty.

The rule of the Sallarids was passed down through Marzuban and Muhammad bin Musafir's descendants until the last Sallarid was killed in 1062, and Seljuk Turks assimilated the dynasty.

The Dynasty of the Ziyarids (CE 931 – 1090)

The Ziyarid dynasty was founded by the Iranian prince Mardavij, who ruled from 930 until 935. Mardavij was born into a Gilanian Zoroastrian family and aimed to create an Iranian Zoroastrian empire like the Sasanian Empire before its defeat by the Muslims. He began his military career by enlisting in the service of his relative Asfar ibn Shiruya. However, Mardavij later betrayed and killed him, taking control of most of Jibal. He then set out to take Hamadan, Dinavar, and Isfahan from the Abbasid Caliphate before pronouncing Isfahan to be the capital of Iran. Finally, in 932, he overcame the military commander of the Daylamite people, Makan ibn Kaki, and took Tabaristan, and by 934, Shiraz and Ahvaz had recognized his sovereignty.

Mardavij was slain in January 935, just before Nowruz celebrations, by his Turkish enslaved people, whom he had mistreated while giving his Daylamite/Gilaki forces preferential treatment. Many of his soldiers joined the Abbasids after his death, while others followed Ali, who established the Buyid dynasty and seized the Mardavij lands in central and southern Iran.

His brother Vushmgir and his Samanid allies led the dynasty in a struggle for territorial dominance against the Buyids. After Vushmgir passed away, his sons Bisutun and Qabus competed for power. In the end, Qabus would outlast his brother and govern the realm. Adud al-Dawla, the ruler of the Buyids, exiled Qabus from 980 to 998, during which time Tabaristan, the center of Ziyarid strength, came to be ruled by him. Early in the 11th century, a slew of further kings took control of the kingdom with Ghaznavid assistance. Finally, the invasion by the Nizari Ismaili state in 1090 brought an end to Ziyarid authority.

The tomb known as the Dome of Qabus, one of Iran's oldest still-standing structures with a date inscription, is one of the Ziyarid dynasty's most well-known architectural accomplishments. The massive brick tomb has a conical roof shaped like a cylinder. Around the circular structure are ten flanges and walls that are ten feet thick and 55 feet in diameter. The entire height is 160 feet. According to the legend, Qabus's body was placed in a glass coffin and suspended from the interior dome of the tower by chains.

The Dynasty of the Buyids (CE 934 – 1062)

From 934 until 1062, the Buyid dynasty ruled over central and southern Iran as well as much of Iraq. They were a Daylamite-descended Shia Iranian dynasty that began with Ali ibn Buya, who destroyed Fars and made Shiraz his capital in 934. His younger brother Hasan ibn Buya acquired control of a piece of Jibal in the late 930s. Ray had been conquered and served as his capital by the year 943. The youngest brother, Ahmad ibn Buya, took over as the country's king in 945 and made Baghdad the capital. He was given the title Mu'izz al-Dawla (Fortifier of the State). Ali, the oldest, was given the title of Imad al-Dawla (Support of the State), while Hasan was given the title of Rukn al-Dawla (Pillar of the State).

The Buyids, who are Daylamite Iranians, deliberately reproduced Sasanian Empire symbols and customs. The customary Sasanian title of Shahanshah, which translates to "king of kings," was initially used by Imad al-Dawla as the monarch of the Buyids. As evidenced by the numerous inscriptions, the Buyids had carved in the Persepolis Achaemenid ruins; they thought the legendary Iranian ruler Jamshid had constructed it.

One of the most notable accomplishments of Adud al-Dawla (who ruled from 949 to 983) is the Band-e Amir in Shiraz, which helped the Buyid dynasty achieve its pinnacle. He governed the Buyid dominion, and it stretched from Syria's western Byzantine boundary to Khorasan's eastern frontiers.

The Buyids first identified as Zaydi Shi'is, but once the twelfth Imam was further occulted in 941, they did so to promote their political objectives. However, the majority of the Buyids in their kingdom were recognized for their adherence to Sunni culture and loyalty to the Sunni Abbasid caliphs. However, they were hostile to the Egyptian Fatimid Isma'ili Caliphate.

The Buyid kingdom was populated mainly by Zoroastrians and Christians, unlike the Samanids, who reigned over a Sunni Muslim populous in Central Asia. As a result, the Buyid period saw a lot of literature in Arabic, Syriac, and Middle Persian. The Buyids were Shi'ites and Twelvers, as were the majority of Daylamites at the period. But they probably started as Zaydis.

Except in situations where it would be politically advantageous, the Buyids rarely tried to impose a specific theological viewpoint on their citizens. While still in control of the caliphate, the Sunni Abbasids lost all secular authority. To avoid conflicts between the Sunnis and the Shia reaching government offices, the Buyid amirs also occasionally employed Christians in place of Muslims from either group.

The Dynasty of the Seljuks (CE 1037 – 1153)

The Muslim Seljuk dynasty, often known as the Seljuk Turks, left an enduring legacy for the medieval Middle East and Central Asia Turco-Persian people. The Persianate status eventually came to them. The

First Crusade was against the Seljuks, who had founded the Sultanate of Rum and the Seljuk Empire. Their empire spanned from Anatolia to Iran at its height. In the eighth century, on the border of the Muslim world, north of the Caspian Sea and the Aral Sea, the Kinik branch of the Oghuz Turks lived in the Oghuz Yabgu State on the Kazakh Steppe of Turkestan.

Due to disagreements with Yabghu, the Oghuz Turks' supreme commander, Seljuk, the clan's leader, broke away from the Oghuz Turks as a whole and established a camp on the western bank of the lower Syr Darya. About 985, the Seljuks made the Islamic faith their own. The Ghaznavids were the first to confront the Seljuks when they arrived in mainland Persia from their homelands in the 11th century. The Seljuks defeated the Ghaznavids at the Battle of Nasa Plains in 1035.

By mixing with the local population and absorbing the Persian language and culture, the Seljuks considerably impacted the development of the Turko-Persian legacy. The members of this dynasty were excellent defenders of Persian literature, art, and culture as a result. The Western Turks, who live in Turkey, Turkmenistan, and Azerbaijan today, are known to have them as forebears.

The "Great Seljuks," who served as the family's head, were supposed to rule over all other Seljuk lineages, but this wasn't always the case. Although the monarch of western Persia was commonly given this title, Turkic tradition requires that the Great Seljuk be the dynasty's senior member.

Under the direction of the sultans Alp-Arslan and Malik-Shah, the Seljuk empire grew to include the entirety of Iran, Mesopotamia, Syria, and Palestine. The Byzantine emperor Romanus IV Diogenes was captured by Alp-Arslan in 1071 at Manzikert after he routed a sizable Byzantine force. Turkmen Seljuks had the option of settling in Asia Minor.

Toghril Beg's triumph over the Buyids in Baghdad in 1055 encouraged Muslim unity under the Sunni caliphate and brought the Seljuks to power. During the Alp-Arslan and Malik expansions to the border with Egypt, the Seljuk vizier Nizam al-Mulk was in charge of the empire's governance. Islam has significantly benefited from the political and theological qualities of the Seljuk dynasty. During the Seljuk era, a network of madrasahs (Islamic colleges) was built, allowing governmental leaders and religious authorities to receive uniform training. The Great Mosque of Esfahan was one of the numerous mosques constructed by the sultans (the Masjed-e Jame). The Seljuk empire saw a flourishing of Persian cultural independence. The Turkmen Seljuks adopted the cultural language of their Persian Islamic professors since they lacked a significant literary tradition or Islamic tradition of their own. As a result, literary Persian flourished over all of Iran, and Arabic became extinct there aside from in works of religious knowledge.

In 1194, the last of the Iranian Seljuks perished in combat, and by 1200 Seljuk rule had all but disappeared outside of Anatolia.

MONGOLS / IL-KHANID DYNASTY (1256 – 1353)

A khanate or kingdom called the Il-Khanid, or Il-Khanate (literally a subordinate khan), was founded in the western part of the Mongol Empire and ruled in Iran from 1256 to 1335. Its primary territory is in what are now parts of Iran, Azerbaijan, and Turkey. At its height, the Il-Khanate also included parts of what are now Iraq, Syria, Armenia,

Georgia, Afghanistan, Turkmenistan, Pakistan, a section of what is now Dagestan, and a bit of what is now Tajikistan. Starting with Ghazan in 1295, later Il-Khanate kings made the Muslim faith their religion. The Black Death destroyed the Il-khanate in the 1330s. The khanate fell apart after Abu Sa'id, the last khan, died in 1335.

Despite not being of Iranian descent, the Il-Khanid kings sought to establish their authority by associating themselves with Iranian history. To this end, they hired historians to portray the Mongols as the successors of the Sasanians (224-651 CE), a pre-Islamic Iranian dynasty.

Religion during the Mongol era was as diverse as the cultural and artistic influences. Despite their belief in shamanism, the Mongols adopted other religions for a variety of reasons, from a personal quest for the spiritual to concerns with control and social and political coherence. In Greater Iran during the Il-Khanid era, Buddhism, Manichaeism, Zoroastrianism, Judaism, Christianity, and Islam were all practiced. Il-Khanid women in the ruling class were primarily Christian. Jews played a vital role in Isfahan and Hamadan and established sizable populations.

THE TIMURID EMPIRE AND OTTOMAN TURKS (1370 – 1508)

A Persianate Turco-Mongol empire that included areas of modern-day Russia, India, Pakistan, Syria, and Turkey was the Timurid Empire, also known as the Gurkani Empire. In addition, the empire reached modern-day Afghanistan, Iraq, Kuwait, Tajikistan, Kazakhstan, and Uzbekistan. It also influenced Iran, the southern Caucasus, Turkmenistan, Tajikistan, and Kazakhstan.

Timur (also known as Tamerlane), a warlord of Turko-Mongol descent, established the empire after Timur's death in 1405. He viewed himself as Genghis Khan's heir and the great restorer of the Mongol Empire. Ma Huan and Chen Cheng, two Chinese ambassadors, frequently traveled to Samarkand in western Asia to buy and trade products. Timur also maintained busy business links with the Golden Horde and Ming China. The Timurid Renaissance began throughout the empire under the mathematician and astronomer Ulugh Begh.

By 1467, the Aq Qoyunlu confederation had overthrown the Timurid dynasty or Timurids entirely. However, the Timurid dynasty retained control over a few emirates in Central Asia and a small region of India. For instance, in the 16th century, the Timurid monarch Babur of Ferghana (modern-day Uzbekistan) conquered Kabulistan (modern-day Afghanistan) and founded a small kingdom. Twenty years later, he used this realm as a staging place for an invasion of India that would lead to the creation of the Mughal Empire.

Timur embarked on a westward journey in 1380, invading several Ilkhanate successor territories. He had driven the Kartids from Herat by the year 1389 and marched into mainland Persia, where he achieved great success. In North India, Timur also achieved many military victories. Under the direction of his grandson Pir Muhammad, he led an army against Multan in 1398, successfully besieging the city for six months. Later that year, Timur led the main force across the Indus River to seize the forts of Loni and Bhatnair, located seven miles northeast of Delhi. Timur triumphantly entered Delhi after defeating Sultan Mahmud Shah's troops in a fight in December 1398. He massacred the populace but spared the artisans, who were moved to Samarkand, his dominion's primary city and administrative hub.

Timur appointed outsiders to some of the significant governorships in the various provinces of his empire and his sons and grandsons to others. After he died in 1405, the family descended into chaos and conflict, and a number of the governorships essentially broke away. By the 1430s, the Qara Qoyunlu had seized control of the Anatolian and Caucasian lands. At the same time, the Timurid emperors remained to rule over the majority of Central Asia, Persia, Mesopotamia, Armenia, and substantial areas of Azerbaijan, Afghanistan, and Pakistan. Samarkand and Herat, which would eventually become the seat of the Timurid Renaissance, functioned as the focus of Persian civilization after the Persian towns had been decimated by battle. Seventeen million people are estimated to have died as a result of Timur's conquests.

The Timurid aristocracy's adoption of Perso-Islamic courtly culture significantly impacted Persian literature, particularly Persian poetry. Persian culture was fostered, especially by Shah Rukh Mirza and his son Mohammad Taragai Olog Beg. The Persian biography of Timur, Zafarnameh, by Sharaf al-Din Ali Yazdi, is one of the most significant pieces of Timurid literature. The basis for this book was a previous Zafarnameh written by Nizam al-Din Shami, who served as Timur's official biographer in his lifetime.

The Timurid emperors actively promoted Islam by erecting mosques and funding academic endeavors, but Muslims have never been the majority within the Mughal Empire. Both Babur and Aurangzeb destroyed temples, occasionally treating non-Muslims harshly. However, Akbar created Din-i-Ilahi, a brand-new monotheistic religion, by fusing Christianity, Hinduism, and Islam. At certain points during their rule, there was a great degree of religious tolerance, and non-Muslims held significant state positions. Non-

Muslims were not punished, and many observed religious holidays following customs other than their own.

The Dynasty Of The Safavids (1500 - 1736)

The Shiite Safavid dynasty caused the Zoroastrians to lose their robust community. Tens of thousands of Zoroastrians and other minorities were killed by the Safavids since it was their policy to force everyone to convert to Shia Islam at the time. As a result, Zoroastrians were not only branded as non-believers but also as impure and social outcasts. If Sunnis refused to convert, they were frequently fined, sent to prison, banished, or killed. Authorities made accusations at the time against Zoroastrians, Armenians, and other minorities who were known for their involvement in the export of spices despite their financial and other problems.

Early in the 16th century, Zoroastrians were transferred to Isfahan, the new capital of Shah Abbas I. The Zoroastrians lived in an area of Isfahan known as Gabr-Mahal, Gabristan, or Gabrabad, all of which are derived from the name 'Gabr,' which was a derogatory epithet for Zoroastrians employed by Muslims and described in records of Europeans who visited his court as being poor and straightforward. Zoroastrians continued to practice their faith but concealed the sacred fires and spoke in Dari, a recently developed dialect, out of fear that Muslims would defile them.

Shah Abbas was a more tolerant monarch than later Safavid kings, allowing the Zoroastrians to live in their prescribed area, albeit as outcasts. However, Zoroastrians were required to convert by Sultan Husayn (1688 – 1728 CE), and those who refused were put to death.

Reports from the Safavid period show that the Shi'ite majority harassed the Zoroastrians and often threatened to destroy their houses of worship. By 1707, the Zoroastrians could no longer openly practice their religion. Nevertheless, many Zoroastrians remained in Isfahan and were coerced into converting to Islam, and by 1821 Gabrabad was in ruins, and there were hardly any Zoroastrians left in the city.

The majority of the Zoroastrian population in Persia left in the late 19th century as a result of increased restrictions placed on them by the Qajar government. Many of them fled to India. Only around 20% of them stayed in isolated communities and mostly hid.

THE AFGHAN INTERLUDE (1722 – 1730)

A period in Iranian history known as the Afghan interlude, which spanned the years 1722–1730, began with an Afghan invasion of Iran and ended with Ashraf's defeat and death.

In 1722, Esfahan, the Safavid capital in Iran, was besieged and taken by Mahmud, a prominent Afghan and former vassal of the Safavids. This effectively ended the Safavid Dynasty and resulted in Shah Soltan-oseyn, the reigning Safavid ruler, being executed by Mahmud in 1723. Mahmud solidified his conquests in southern and southeastern Iran, and his cousin Ashraf took over as ruler in 1725. Despite Ashraf's efforts to appease the Iranians, they always saw him as a despised foreign invader.

In the meantime, Peter the Great of Russia invaded the north of Iran in 1722, reportedly due to losses experienced by some Russian merchants during a tribal rebellion there, but Peter the Great had long wished to build a trade route to India via the nation east of the Caspian Sea. The Ottomans went into western and northern Iran to stop the

Russians from occupying Iranian territory near Turkey. Despite the conflict's potential to escalate into war, a compromise was eventually reached in 1724. The northwest areas of Iran were divided between Russia and the Ottomans, who controlled most of Iran's north and west, respectively. This was possibly the first time that European powers imposed such specific borders on an Islamic state.

The Safavid Dynasty's representative Tahmasp II ruled over the provinces of Mazandaran and Gilan in the north. As part of a pact he struck with the Ottomans in 1727, Ashraf agreed to let them annex western Iran in exchange for the Ottomans recognizing Ashraf as Iran's king. The head of the Afshar tribe, Nadir Qoli Khan, joined Tahmasp II in 1727. Nadir, who eventually ruled as Nadir Shah from 1736 to 1747, set out to drive the Afghans out and reunite the erstwhile Safavid realms. Nadir, a superb general, murdered Ashraf and placed Tahmasp II as shah in Esfahan after defeating the Afghans in a series of battles (1729). He persisted in his efforts against the Afghans until 1730, when the Afghan people were eventually driven out of Iran.

NADIR SHAH (1736 – 1747)

The Iranian conquistador and monarch Nadir Shah founded an empire that spanned from the Indus River to the Caucasus Mountains. Nadir belonged to the obscure Safavid shahs of the Iran-supporting Turkic Afshar tribe. Nadr established and controlled a gang of robbers while exhibiting strong leadership qualities after working for a local chieftain. He led 5,000 bandits in 1726 to aid Safavid king Tahmasp II in his bid to retake the throne his father had lost to Ghilzay Afghan usurper Mahmud four years earlier. In a series of great victories, Nadir defeated the Ghilzay Afghans and returned Tahmasp II to the Iranian throne while rebuilding Iran's military forces.

Soon after Tahmasp II was returned to the throne, he attempted to invade the Turks but was quickly defeated and forced to sign a peace treaty. Nadir was incensed by this, so he hurried back, deposed Tahmasp II, but the latter's infant son in charge, and proclaimed himself regent. By ultimately driving the Turks out of Iran, Nadir exacted retribution on them. Later, by threatening Russia with war, he convinced that nation to hand up control of its Caspian regions to Iran. Finally, the Safavid dynasty, which had ruled Iran for more than 200 years before Tahmasp II's son Abbas III's overthrow in 1736, was deposed by Nadir Shah, who had ascended to the Iranian throne under the name Nadir Shah.

Thanks to the navy he kept building, Nadir Shah was able to seize Bahrain from the Arabs as well as invade and conquer Oman. In February 1739, he attacked the main Mughal army in Karnal, India, after taking many Mughal cities in northern India. The Koh-i-noor diamond and the majestic Peacock Throne were among the enormous amount of treasure he brought back to Iran after conquering Delhi and winning the battle. When he began fighting the Uzbeks between Bukhara and Khiva, his empire had reached its peak in size and was second only to the ancient Iranian empires in size. Nadir held the Central Asian rulers Timur and Genghis Khan in high regard. He modeled his military prowess after them and their brutality, especially later in his rule. A large empire that included Iran, the North Caucasus, Armenia, Turkmenistan, Azerbaijan, Georgia, Turkey, Iraq, Afghanistan, and Uzbekistan, as well as Oman, Bahrain, Pakistan, and the Persian Gulf at its height, was developed as a result of his numerous military endeavors. However, his military spending had a terrible effect on Iran's economy.

Nadir Shah had his eldest son blinded after an attempt on his life in 1741 failed because he thought he was involved. Additionally, he made an effort to convert Iran's primarily Shi'ite populace to Sunni Islam. Nadir Shah once more fought the Ottoman Turks in 1743, but uprisings in Iran compelled him to reach a truce. However, he reopened hostilities with the Turks as soon as he could, defeating them decisively close to Yerevan. Finally, in 1746, peace was declared.

Nadir Shah was an excellent soldier and general, but he lacked leadership and management skills, which led to Iran's complete exhaustion in his later years of rule. Tens of thousands of people died as a result of his never-ending wars, and his tax collectors' extortions ruined the nation's economy. Although Nadir Shah had always been stern and cunning, these qualities got more robust with age. Everywhere he went, he had individuals tortured and put to death because of his growing suspicion and arbitrary cruelty. As a result, he was the target of a revolt. In the end, he was killed by his soldiers when putting down a rebellion in Khorasan. Nadir Shah had no interests outside fighting and conquering. When told that paradise was free from conflict, he once quipped, "How then can there be any delights there?"

Shi'ism was imposed as Iran's official religion by the Safavids. Nadir has likely raised in the Shi'a faith. Still, when he gained power and began to annex the Ottoman Empire, he changed to Sunni Islam because he believed Safavid Shi'ism was to blame for the intensified war with the Sunni Ottoman Empire. Shi'a and Sunni Muslims comprised a portion of his army (with a noticeable minority of Christians and Kurds). He thought that a kind of Shi'ism he dubbed "Ja'fari" in honor of the sixth Shi'a imam Ja'far al-Sadiq would be more acceptable to Sunni Muslims. He also prohibited Shi'a customs, such as cursing the first three caliphs of Islam, that were particularly objectionable to Sunni

Muslims. However, Nadir's friend, a French Jesuit, asserted that it was challenging to determine which faith he adhered to and that many individuals who knew him well stated that he had none. Nadir is said to have had a neutral attitude toward religion and frequently took funds intended for the Shi'a clergy and used them instead to fund his army.

THE DYNASTY OF THE ZANDS (1751 – 1779)

Karim Khan Zand, who ruled Iran from 1751 to 1779, established the Zand dynasty. In the 18th century, they first ruled over parts of southern and central Iran. Later, except for the provinces of Balochistan and Khorasan, it expanded to include the majority of remaining modern-day Iran as well as portions of Iraq. In addition, modern-day Armenia, Azerbaijan, and Georgia were governed by khanates that were technically a part of the Zand monarchy but functionally independent. The independent Al-Mazkur sheikhdom of Bushire also ruled the island of Bahrain for the Zands.

Karim Khan ruled at a time of wealth and peace. Karim Khan's dominion saw a blossoming of the arts and architecture, with Shiraz as its capital. Some of the building's structural elements were copied from surrounding monuments from the Sasanian (224-651 CE) and Achaemenid (550-330 BCE) eras of pre-Islamic Iran. Karim Khan also restored the tombs of the classical Persian poets Saadi Shirazi and Hafez. Later, Qajar's arts and crafts were influenced by the peculiar Zand artwork produced at the rulers' orders.

Karim Khan is still regarded as the most compassionate Iranian emperor of the Islamic era, even though Zand Iran collapsed after his death as a result of feuding among the dynasty's members. Political implications resulted from the Zands' decision to refer to themselves as

Vakilol Ro'aya (Advocate of the People), notably Karim Khan. In addition to its obvious propaganda value, the title may also reflect the aspirations of the time, which were for popularly inclined rulers as opposed to absolute monarchs who were wholly cut off from the populace, like the earlier Safavids.

Shiraz was designated as Karim Khan's capital, while Tehran was added as the second capital in 1778, and thus he took over the southern and central regions of Iran. To prove his claim, Karim Khan put the young Shah Ismail III, the last Safavid king's grandson, on the throne in 1757. However, Ismail was only a de facto ruler; Karim Khan held absolute control. Many of Karim Khan's most well-known structures, such as the Arg of Karim Khan, the Vakil Bazaar, and numerous mosques and gardens, can be seen in Shiraz. He is also in charge of constructing the Tehran palace, where the Qajar dynasty will eventually reside.

After Karim Khan died in 1779, his enemies were able to put his realm in danger. Unfortunately, other rulers did not follow Karim Khan's ideals, and the nation soon came under attack from all directions. The Qajar chiefs were the worst opponents and were moving quickly against the ailing state. Although Lotf Ali Khan, Karim Khan's grandnephew, proclaimed himself the new king in 1789, most of his rule (which lasted till 1794) was devoted to fighting the Qajar chiefs. The Zand Dynasty was all but over when Lotif Ali Khan was ultimately apprehended and brutally murdered in the castle of Bam.

Karim Khan had the same moderate religious beliefs as many tribal chiefs, but he also accepted Shi'ite practices and coined the term Hujjat Allah al-Mahdi, the Twelver Shia Mahdi. Unlike the Safavids, Karim Khan did not seek the approval of the clergy for political decisions. He is said to have been very tolerant of those who practiced religions other than Islam, not interfering with religious freedom.

THE DYNASTY OF THE QAJARS (1789 - 1925)

Mulla Gushtasp, a Zoroastrian astrologer, foresaw the Zand dynasty's demise at the hands of the Qajar forces at Kerman. The Zoroastrians of Kerman were spared by Agha Mohammad Khan Qajar's conquest force as a result of Gushtasp's prophecy.

Nevertheless, the Zoroastrian population continued to suffer throughout the Qajar era, and their numbers continued to decline. Many Zoroastrians were killed even under the leadership of the dynasty's founder, Agha Mohammad Khan, and some of them were taken as enslaved people to Azerbaijan. As a result, the Qajar period is regarded by Zoroastrians as being among the worst.

Many contemporary documents comment on the persecution of Zoroastrians and the fact that fear of Muslim fanatics was always foremost in the minds of Zoroastrians. They thought that their lives were in jeopardy whenever the aggressive spirit of Islam manifested, and this was often correct. During this time, it is noted that Zoroastrian homes had to have lower walls than Muslim homes, and they were not allowed to display any distinguishing symbols on them. Additionally, Zoroastrians were prohibited from building new homes and making any repairs to existing ones.

Zoroastrian people were subjected to a variety of racial prejudices and prohibitions. The neighborhoods where Zoroastrian people lived were seen as unclean, and they were treated as outcasts. Many public establishments refused to serve Zoroastrians because they were regarded as unclean, and the food they ate was considered unclean.

They were forbidden from touching any food or fruit while they were shopping in the bazaar. They frequently had their religious shrines desecrated, were beaten severely, and faced threats of being coerced into conversion. Persecutions and harassment were commonplace in daily life. Muslims frequently attacked and beat Zoroastrians in the streets. Zoroastrians who were murdered received no justice. Zoroastrian females were occasionally kidnapped and coerced into becoming Muslims.

Due to dress regulations that forbade them from donning fresh or white clothing and mandated them to wear a soft yellow robe as a distinguishing mark, the Zoroastrian people were also subjected to racial hatred. Even though it was chilly outdoors, they had to wear long qaba robes and cotton geeveh on their feet because they were not permitted to wear coats. Zoroastrians were not allowed to carry watches or jewelry or wear pants, headgear, boots, socks, or long cloaks. Because the water seeped through their clothing and bodies could taint the Muslims, they were prohibited from carrying umbrellas and walking outside in the rain. When visiting a Muslim home in Yazd, Zoroastrian men would grab a sizable shawl and place it beneath their feet to prevent contaminating the carpet. They were only permitted to ride mules or donkeys; they were not permitted to ride horses, and they had to dismount before a Muslim.

The Zoroastrians had to endure numerous hardships in addition to paying a hefty religious fee known as Jizya. Zoroastrian writings claim that because the dhimmi had to stand while the official receiving the money sat on a regal throne, this taxation system intended to degrade the dhimmi. The officer gave the dhimmi money, then kicked him in the neck and obnoxiously pulled away. The public was encouraged to view the show. Arab tax collectors would make fun of

Zoroastrians wearing Kushtis before removing them and subjugating its adherents by tying the thread around their necks. Every intermediary had to take a share because the tax authority was corrupt, and occasionally, the official amount would be collected two or three times. The children were harassed and occasionally tortured, and governors would set their religious belongings on fire if the family could not pay the Jizya. This approach gave rise to the phrase "the bookless." Due to horrifying conditions, some people were compelled to convert, while others pretended to be Muslims and took Muslim names while yet covertly holding onto Zoroastrian beliefs. The latter Zoroastrians are now referred to as Jaddids. The Zoroastrian community grew isolated, stagnant, and closed off as a result of discrimination and persecution.

Since the discrimination against Zoroastrians was so pervasive during the Qajar Dynasty, many Zoroastrians took this opportunity to flee Iran for India. For years, the Zoroastrian community in Iran had contacts in the Parsi community of India. As a result, many of the Parsi community donated money and resources to help their Iranian brethren escape from Iran.

THE PAHLAVIS AND THE IRANIAN REVOLUTION (1925 – 1979)

Beginning in the early 20th century, all Iranian communities quickly migrated to Tehran, the nation's capital. By 1912, there were reported to be 500 Zoroastrians, up from roughly 50 reported in 1881. Zoroastrians transitioned from being one of Iran's most persecuted minorities to becoming a representation of Iranian nationality during the Pahlavi dynasty.

The Pahlavi monarchy, commanded by Shah Mohammad Reza Pahlavi, was ousted during the Iranian Revolution, which resulted in the foundation of an Islamic republic under the leadership of Ayatollah Ruhollah Khomeini, the leader of one of the factions in the rebellion. The revolt was backed by numerous leftist and Islamist organizations.

Pahlavi joined forces with the Western Bloc and the United States to create a more authoritarian monarchy following the 1953 Iranian coup d'état. He leaned significantly on American backing to maintain his position of power, in which he remained for an additional 26 years. This sparked the White Revolution in 1963, which resulted in Ayatollah Khomeini's detention and exile in 1964. Demonstrations started in October 1977 amid intense hostilities between Khomeini and the Shah, growing into a secular and religious civil opposition movement. The destruction of the Rex Theater, which was the start of the revolution, sparked a swift upsurge in protests in 1978, and from August until December of that year, strikes and rallies crippled the nation.

The 1979 Revolution, also known as the Islamic Revolution, began in January 1978 with the first big anti-Shah demonstrations. After a year of protests and rioting that rendered the country and its economy useless, Mohammad Reza Pahlavi escaped to the US. In February 1979, when Ruhollah Khomeini returned from exile, he installed a new government in Tehran. In response to a vote, Iran proclaimed itself an Islamic republic in April 1979. After a second vote, a theocratic constitution was approved in December 1979.

The first statewide uprisings against the new government began with the 1979 Kurdish revolt, which was followed by uprisings in Khuzestan, Sistan, Baluchestan, and other provinces. Over the following years, these uprisings were brutally put to a stop by the new

Islamic government. The recently installed regime was expelling both the moderate Islamist political opposition and the political opposition led by non-Islamists. Islamists, nationalists, and Marxists joined forces to oust the Shah, but the new government was responsible for slaughtering tens of thousands of people. Khomeini's order to purge the new government of everyone still supporting the exiled Shah led to the execution of numerous former ministers and members of the cabinet, including former prime minister Amir-Abbas Hoveyda.

On November 4, 1979, a group of Muslim students took the American Embassy and held 52 employees and citizens hostage after the US refused to extradite Mohammad Reza Pahlavi to the new government. The Jimmy Carter administration's fruitless negotiations to gain the hostages' release and an unsuccessful attempt to rescue them contributed to Carter's declining popularity among American voters, ultimately leading to his ouster from office and the election of Ronald Reagan. The Algiers Accords allowed for the release of the last hostages on Jimmy Carter's last day in office. Mohammad Reza Pahlavi departed for Egypt before passing away on July 27, 1980, from cancer-related symptoms.

On January 16, 1979, The Shah, the last Persian king, abdicated and fled Iran for exile, ceding authority to a regency council and a prime minister supported by the opposition. Ayatollah Khomeini was invited by the authorities to return, and when he did, he was welcomed in Tehran by a large crowd of Iranians. However, the regal era came to an end shortly after, on February 11, when guerrillas and rebel forces engaged Shah-aligned soldiers in armed street fights, ushering in Khomeini as the nation's rightful ruler. On April 1, 1979, Iran opted to establish an Islamic republic through a national referendum. In addition, a new theocratic-republican constitution was created and adopted; in December of the same year, Khomeini was chosen as the nation's supreme leader.

The revolution stood out because it astonished people all across the world. It occurred in a very wealthy country, brought about considerable change rapidly, was hugely popular, drove many Iranians into exile, and replaced a pro-Western, secular, authoritarian monarchy with an anti-Western, theocratic government founded on the velayat-e f principle. Many of the standard catalysts for revolution were absent (loss in a war, peasant rebellion, financial crisis, or an unsatisfied military). In addition, the revolution sought to restore Shia Islam throughout the Middle East and topple the region's predominately Arab Sunni government.

THE ISLAMIC REPUBLIC OF IRAN (1979-PRESENT)

The Zoroastrian people suffered during the 1979 Islamic Revolution, which resulted in a sharp decline in their population. Shortly after the revolution, under Bazargan's rule, it is said that Muslim revolutionaries broke into one of Tehran's prominent Zoroastrian fire temples, and Ayatollah Khomeini's image was put in place of the Prophet Zoroaster in temples.

The Iran-Iraq War, which started in September 1980 when the Iraqi army seized the western Iranian province of Khuzestan, is evidence that the revolution was never really over. Despite some early victories for Saddam Hussein's forces, Iranian forces had successfully driven the Iraqi army back into Iraq by the middle of 1982. The Iranian leadership decided to invade Iraq in July 1982 and launched numerous offensives to take over Iraqi territory and seize cities like Basra while

Iraq was put on the defensive. After routing Iranian forces within Iraq, the Iraqi army forced them back across the border, ending the battle in 1988. Khomeini then agreed to a cease-fire brokered by the UN. According to estimates, between 123,220 and 160,000 military personnel died during the conflict in Iran, along with 11,000 and 16,000 civilians.

Following the Iran-Iraq War in 1989, Akbar Hashemi Rafsanjani and his government concentrated on a pragmatic and pro-business economic strategy while remaining mainly true to the revolution's goals of strengthening and rebuilding the economy. In 1997, a moderate reformist named Mohammad Khatami succeeded Rafsanjani. However, his administration made fruitless attempts to advance democracy and freedom in the country.

Mahmoud Ahmadinejad, a conservative populist contender, won the 2005 presidential election and came to office. According to the Interior Ministry, Mir-Hossein Mousavi came in second place behind incumbent President Ahmadinejad, who earned 62.63 percent of the vote in the 2009 Iranian presidential election with 33.75 percent of the vote. Long-lasting demonstrations after the hotly contested election resulted in critical cities both inside and outside of Iran and led to the founding of the Iranian Green Movement.

Hassan Rouhani won the presidential election on June 15, 2013, besting Mohammad Bagher Ghalibaf and four other candidates. However, little has changed in Iran's ties with its neighbors as a result of Rouhani's victory.

Between 2017 and 2018, nationwide protests against the country's longtime Supreme Leader and the government broke out in Iran as a result of the country's economic and political circumstances. It was confirmed in writing that a large number of protesters were imprisoned. The nationwide protests were significant in both magnitude and scope. On November 15, 2019, in Ahvaz, the 2019–20 Iranian demonstrations got underway. When the government proposed fuel price increases of up to 300 percent, they swiftly swept across the country. Several international observers, including Amnesty International, claim that during the bloodiest government crackdown on protestors in the Islamic Republic's history, thousands of people were detained, and hundreds were killed within a short period. When the entire country's Internet was shut down for a week, it was one of the worst Internet blackouts ever recorded.

Tensions between the two countries were at an all-time high by the time the US executed Qasem Soleimani, the revolutionary guard general, in Iraq on January 3, 2020. Three days later, Iran's Islamic Revolutionary Guard Corps accidentally brought down Ukraine International Airlines Flight 752, killing 176 civilians and sparking widespread discontent throughout the nation while attacking US troops in Iraq. The government ultimately confirmed the surface-to-air missile shootdown of the aircraft as the outcome of an international probe after three days of denial and calling it a "human error."

Along with the Armenian, Assyrian, and Persian Jewish populations, Zoroastrianism is currently recognized as one of Iran's official religions. Zoroastrian representatives are permitted to take the floor at least once in the Iranian Parliament. Out-marriage and low birth rates have an impact on the expansion of Iran's Zoroastrian community, which, according to the results of the 2012 census, is still at 25,271 despite a population increase of 27.5 percent from that of 2006. Sepanta Niknam, the first Zoroastrian politician in modern Iran, was elected to the Yazd municipal council in 2013.

MIGRATION TO INDIA (10TH TO 20TH CENTURIES)

Throughout the Islamic era, numerous waves of Zoroastrians immigrated to India. The initial departure after the conquest was described as a result of Muslim invaders' religious persecution. According to the story, after experiencing suffering at their hands, the Zoroastrians fled, first to northern Iran, then to the island of Hormuz, and last to India, to defend themselves and uphold their faith. This well-known migrant story emphasizes the persecution of Muslims and labels Parsis as religious refugees.

Academics lately questioned the claim that Zoroastrians were of Iranian descent as they were already well-established in India during the Sasanian era. According to the legend, the Zoroastrians fled, first to northern Iran, then to the island of Hormuz, and last to India, to defend themselves and keep their faith after suffering at their hands. This well-known migrant narrative highlights Muslim oppression and characterizes Parsis as religious refugees.

Zoroastrians were already well-established in India during the Sasanian era, leading academics to recently contest the assertion that they were of Iranian descent. Legend has it that at the beginning of the 10th century, a small group of Zoroastrians met at Nyshapour and the Fort of Sanjan and decided that Iran was no longer a safe location for Zoroastrians and their religion. Before any severe persecution, they may have migrated due to competition with Muslims for trading routes.

According to Parsi lore, local culture is effortlessly incorporated, except for two incidents in the Qissa. West India is home to the world's largest Zoroastrian community, which is still growing. According to Parsi mythology, their ancestors fled the oppressive dictatorship of the fanatical Muslim conquerors to India while adhering to their traditional religion. The epic poem Qissa-i-Sanjan describes the early years of Zoroastrian settlement on the Indian subcontinent (Story of Sanjan). The severity of the repression that the Parsis' ancestors experienced in Iran has only recently come to light.

The Parsis flourished in their new country, and after learning about the Qajar dynasty's persecution of Zoroastrians in Iran, they organized funds to assist them. Agents were dispatched to Iran, but they only discovered about 7,000 Zoroastrians in Kerman, Yazd, and Tehran. Nevertheless, he was able to get some of the Zoroastrians' persecution eased thanks to his connections with the British administration. The Persian Zoroastrian Amelioration Fund put pressure on the Qajar government to eliminate jizya, which the Zoroastrian minority had been paying up until 1882.

The Zoroastrian Trust Funds of Europe (ZTFE) helped to improve the quality of life for displaced Zoroastrians. Dadabhai Naoroji and Mancherjee Bhownagree discussed the persecution of Zoroastrians in Iran in the UK House of Commons in their respective capacities as presidents of the ZTFE and elected lawmakers. At the time, Shah Naser al-Din Shah Qajar was visiting London. Parsi ZTFE leaders were there to defend their Iranian counterpart religious activists who had endured dreadful persecution under the Qajar regime.

PERSECUTION OF ZOROASTRIANS

Zoroastrianism has a long history of discrimination against its adherents. Zoroastrians were subjected to particularly widespread persecution after the seventh century CE when Islam first appeared; during and after Arab Muslims' conquest of Persia, Zoroastrians faced prejudice and harassment, including sporadic acts of violence and forced conversions. Zoroastrian temples are said to have been demolished by Muslims who came to the area after the Rashidun Caliphate annexed it. In addition, Zoroastrians who lived in Muslim-ruled territories had to pay a levy known as jizya.

It is reported that the Muslims torched many Persian libraries, and Persian cultural heritage was significantly damaged during this time. The Muslims also regulated Zoroastrian activity, and their ability to participate in society was constrained by an increasing number of regulations that the Rashidun Caliphate enacted. As a result, Muslims started to harass Zoroastrians more frequently and harshly over time, which led to Zoroastrians dying or converting, which in turn contributed to the religion's downfall. A large number of Zoroastrians fled to India and were given refuge as Islamization started to spread throughout Persia under Muslim authority. Many Zoroastrians took the perilous voyage to India because of the severity of the oppression and poverty. Those who could not afford to travel on the ships risked their lives by riding donkeys or even walking over the dangerous desert. On their journey, they were protected by their Parsi brothers in India, who provided money, food, and shelter where they could.

Zoroastrians were reportedly massacred later during the Qajar Dynasty, in many cities, including two massacres reported in the towns of Turkabad and Boarzjan. The Zoroastrian surnames Turk, Turki, Turkian, and Turkabadi indicate ancestry to the Turkabad survivors, and locals still refer to the nearby village of Maul Seyyed Aul as a "death site" (Ghatl-Gauh). In 1850 in Iran, there were only an estimated 6000 Zoroastrians remaining.

To avoid prejudice and the unpleasant consequences of being treated like second-class citizens under the caliphates, many Zoroastrians converted to Islam. Zoroastrianism's decline was hastened by the process of moving the children of Zoroastrian subjects to an Islamic school where they would study Arabic, the Qur'an, and other holy texts. The Persian language, however, made a remarkable comeback and flourished during the Samanid Empire at the start of the Iranian Intermezzo.

Zoroastrians were awarded dhimmi status following the Muslim invasion of Persia and were subject to persecution throughout Iran. Discrimination and harassment began as isolated incidents of violence that police and legislators ignored. The tax collectors humiliated and insulted those who paid the Jizya, though those who didn't pay were often subject to violence against themselves, their families, or their property. Many Zoroastrians were captured as enslaved people during this time. They were only set free if they embraced Islam.

According to legend, many religious buildings at Istakhr, Bukhara, and other Persian cities were transformed from fire temples into mosques by adding a mihrab (prayer niche) to the part of the arch closest to Mecca. The inhabitants of the urban districts where Arab administrators had settled had to either adopt Islam culture or leave. The number of rules governing Zoroastrian behavior gradually expanded, restricting their participation in society and making their lives challenging. The expectation that they would convert to Islam when being a Zoroastrian became too difficult. To some extent, this worked, as the number of adherents fell sharply with increased persecution. Many people changed religions to escape the institutionalized prejudice and injustice enforced by the law of the land, while some did so only briefly.

Others converted to Islam. After all, under Zoroastrian beliefs, their employment in industry and artisanal labor would render them unclean because their profession involved defiling fire. Because the two faiths shared many inherent principles, Muslim missionaries had little trouble conveying them to Zoroastrians. Ahriman and Ahura Mazda would seem to the Persian like Allah and Iblis.

Some people question the severity of the Zoroastrians' forced conversions to Islam, pointing to numerous instances of the Muslim conquerors' tolerance and coming to the conclusion that it is impossible to exclusively blame the decline of Zoroastrianism on the violent conversions carried out by the Muslim conquerors. The parallels between the two religions may have motivated some Zoroastrians to convert, and some conversions appeared sincere. In addition, Islam offered a more comprehensive range of brotherhood as opposed to the constricting Zoroastrian standards. However, there are documented cases of persecution of Zoroastrians, and evidence of Parsi migration to India can be found throughout history, from the Muslim conquest of 633 BCE through to the 20th century during the Qajar Dynasty.

Nevertheless, Islam is not the only thing to blame for the demise of Zoroastrianism. Even after the conquest, significant Jewish and Nestorian Christian populations were still in the city of Nishapur. Moreover, the Iranian nobility that resided there either made agreements with the believers to gain nearly total autonomy over the territory in exchange for a tribute tax or jizyah, or the northern was barely penetrated by the "believers" for a century because Zoroastrians continued to live in these areas in significant numbers long after Islam's spread there.

Persecution by Christians

Not just Muslims and Islam were to blame for the persecution of Zoroastrians. During the protracted battle between the Roman Empire and Persia, those Zoroastrians who lived in Asia Minor under Christian rule endured agony. Christians who resided in Sassanian-controlled areas are said to have destroyed numerous fire temples and Zoroastrian temples. Christian priests deliberately put out the sacred fire of the Zoroastrians, who also denigrated them as worshippers of the evil Zardusht (Zoroaster), who served false gods and the elements.

OFFSHOOTS OF ZOROASTRIANISM

Mazdakism

One Iranian religion, Mazdakism, was a branch of Zoroastrianism, in which the belief system has been cited as a notable manifestation of pre-modern communism. Zardusht, a Zoroastrian mobad who lived during the early Sasanian Empire created the faith, however, it bears the name of Mazdak, its most well-known supporter and a significant person under Emperor Kavad I.

Mazdakism was a dualistic faith that seems to have Manichaean roots. It advocated the idea that the cosmos was created when two opposing principles, those of light and dark or good and evil merged. The Mazdakites revered the God of Light.

Mazdakism vigorously encouraged pacifist and austere living. Murder, the use of animals for food or sport, and the consumption of meat were all prohibited. All persons, including their opponents, were to be treated generously by followers. To curb avarice, the movement also promoted group marriage and polyandry (where one woman has multiple husbands), the latter of which, if real, was probably encouraged because there were few women available for poor men to marry due to the polygamy of the higher classes in Iranian society at the time.

In the latter part of the fifth century, Mazdakism gained popularity in Iran as it was seen as a reform movement that sought a positive interpretation of Manichaean dualism. A connection has been made between its founder, Zaradust-e Khuragan, and a Persian named Bundos. At the close of the third century, they preached a variant Manichaeism in Rome under Diocletian. After the fifth century, the religion's primary Persian proponent, Mazdak, became known as the religion in general. Although Mazdakite literature is extinct, the movement has been mentioned briefly in Syrian, Persian, Arabic, and Greek sources.

Good (or Light) and Evil (or Darkness) are the two initial principles of Mazdakism. Darkness behaves haphazardly and without free will; light behaves intentionally and freely. The world was created after the two were unintentionally combined. The three components of Light are the elements of water, fire, and earth. The worshipped god of Light is seated on a paradise throne and endowed with the four faculties of perception, intelligence, memory, and joy. The 12 signs of the zodiac and the seven old planets are represented by the 12 spiritual animals and seven viziers that Good rules over. The seven and 12 rule the planet, and the four powers are combined in man.

People who followed Mazdakism were taught to strive to spread the Light via their deeds; this is done by moral behavior and an austere lifestyle. They are not to consume the flesh and are to treat enemies with kindness, hospitality, and compassion. Mazdak aimed to promote fraternal cooperation and lessen factors that lead to avarice and conflict. Kavadh I of the Sassanid Dynasty was converted to this faith and instituted social reforms based on its principles. These reforms appear to have involved some easing of the restrictions governing marriage and property measures. Unfortunately, the social reforms that were instituted incited the hatred of the orthodox Zoroastrian clergy and the noble class, ultimately resulting in Mazdakism's downfall. However, the faith persisted in secrecy into Islamic times (the 8th century).

The Zoroastrian hierarchy considered Mazdakism to be a heretical religion, and Zoroastrian and Sassanian leaders persecuted its adherents. Finally, in about 524 BCE, Khosrau I, the Sassanian king, began an offensive against the Mazdakis. They were all slaughtered in a massacre that restored traditional Zoroastrianism as the state religion. The massacre claimed the lives of many of the Mazdakian worshipers, including Mazdak himself.

There are numerous ways to characterize the manner of dying. For instance, to give Mazdak the impression of a "human garden," some accounts claim that Mazdak was shot multiple times while hanging upside down. However, other sources claim that the three thousand Mazdakis were buried alive with their feet up. Alternative accounts depict a lot more heinous ways to die. Anushiravan then began implementing his own significant administrative and social changes. Following the massacre, Mazdakism was all but extinct. Muslims have occasionally supported Zoroastrian clergy in battles against Zoroastrians that the Zoroastrian clergy saw as heretics or separatists, such as the Mazdakis, in the past.

The Parsi Religion

The word Parsi translates to "Persian" in the Persian language. The Parsi people were Zoroastrian in origin, who left Iran for various reasons and continued to practice a form of Zoroastrianism in India. Tradition holds that the first Parsi people left Persia after the Muslims conquered the Sassanid Dynasty. However, the migration appears to have persisted through to the 20th century, and there is evidence of a Parsi community in India before the end of the Sassanid Dynasty.

As they established communities in India, the Parsi people were able to maintain many of their traditions while also integrating into Indian society and developing many of their unique traditions.

The main difference between Zoroastrians and Parsi is the difference in the calendars that they use. Because the original calendar had 360 days, rather than 360¼ days as in our modern Gregorian calendar, the days slowly drifted from the Zoroastrian communities, who later added leap days to their calendars. As a result, the two calendars are approximately five months out of synch with Nowroz (New Year), happening either in March or in August, depending on which calendar is followed.

The main religious tenants of Parsi are the same as Zoroastrianism, as they are effectively the same religion. However, since the Parsi people have lived in India for hundreds of years, they have adopted some Indian cultural practices in terms of food, dress, and habits. In essence, all Parsi people are Zoroastrian, but not all Zoroastrian people are Parsi since Parsi identifies a specific group of Iranian people who migrated to India for religious freedom.

THE PARSI-MUSLIM RIOTS

The Parsi-Muslim riots first broke out in Bombay in 1851, and they returned to some areas of Gujarat in 1874. These signaled the start of a time of conflict between the two communities.

The first brawl broke out in October 1851 over a blurry print of the Islamic prophet Muhammad that appeared in the Chitra Gyan Darpan, a Parsi newspaper, and it lasted for a month. The article was displayed on the Jama Masjid wall in Bombay and written in the Parsi daily Chitra Gyan Darpan. Islam forbids the representation of Muhammad in pictures, so when people saw it as they were leaving the mosque after Namaz (about 11 a.m.), they became furious. In addition, Muhammad appeared to be blind in one eye because the printer mistakenly printed an image of him with a spot covering one of his eyes.

The crowd attacked Parsis in their homes and on the streets. The aggressors took jewelry, ransacked Zoroastrian fire temples, and pillaged stores. The kotwal attempted to put an end to the disturbances but was unsuccessful. The police could not stop the violence. A curfew was set to try to keep the people apart, and troops were stationed throughout the city.

In a meeting with representatives from both faiths one month later, on November 24, 1851, Cursetji made it clear that the goal of the depiction of the prophet of Islam was not to offend Muslims. He clarified that it was merely some facts about Muhammad, just like all the other noteworthy people the journal was used to reporting. He said that Simon Ockley was the source of the contentious work. Sir Jamsetjee Jeejeebhoy and the Kazi of Bombay traveled together in the same carriage through Muslim and Parsi neighborhoods to show kindness and camaraderie and that the two cultures could coexist happily.

A second riot broke out in May 1857 after some Muslims accused a Parsi named Bejonji Sheriaiji Bharucha of disrespecting a mosque in Bharuch. Bharuch was a significant commerce hub on India's west coast where there were a sizable number of Parsis because it was a historic Parsi community. One of the first priests to settle in Bharuch was Zanhosht Mowbed's younger brother, Bahram, who oversaw the building of a tower of silence in 1309.

Over 200 Muslims gathered in the town's northernmost Bawa Rahan shrine after five days. The police tried to disperse the crowd but were unsuccessful. Ervad Ardeshir Hormazdji Kamdin, the temple of fire Dastur Kamdin Dar-e Mihr's High Priest, was assassinated by the mob. Bejonji Sheriaiji Bharucha was lynched, carrying his corpse through the streets. During the onslaught, they also hurt Ervad Meherwanji Muncherji Kamdin, the High Priest of the Shapurji Narielwala Fire Temple (consecrated in 1783). The nearby towns of Vagra, Amod, Ankleshwar, and Hansot supplied the troops to help soothe the crowd.

Out of 61 people who were detained, 39 received prison sentences from Sessions Judge Alexander Kinloch Forbes. Two people were executed for the murders of Bharucha and the High Priest.

On February 13, 1874, a third riot broke out over a chapter on Muhammad's life in a book called Famous Prophets and Communities. Muhammad was just one of several famous people whose biographies were included in a Gujarati book written by Rustomjee Hormusjee Jalbhoy. When the Muslim people discovered this, they formed mobs and began to attack Parsis. It was recorded that the mobs were hitting

Parsis in their homes and on the streets with no resistance. At Khetwadi, riots broke out once more the following day. A Muslim funeral procession was being led towards a cemetery when some Parsis started hurling stones at it the next day. At Jamsetjee Hospital, where numerous other injured people were also being treated, four Parsis and seven Muslims were admitted.

On November 26, 1885, there was yet another riot between Muslims and Parsis because the government had refused to provide them a plot of land on which to erect a Dargah. They were accused of not granting this since the Municipal Council had Parsi members who were suppressing the Muslim community members.

CHAPTER 5
WHAT IS IT LIKE TODAY?

CURRENT DISTRIBUTION OF ZOROASTRIANS

When the Sasanian Empire was conquered and overthrown by the Arabs, Zoroastrianism continued to thrive for a time, particularly in Iran's rural areas, until the invasions of the Turks and the Mongols in the eleventh and thirteenth centuries. Only then did Zoroastrians flee en masse to Kerman and Yazd, two desert towns. Many Zoroastrians left Iran for the Indian subcontinent immediately after the Arab invasion of Iran in 651 CE. They established themselves there, adopted the name Parsis, and developed into a sizeable minority while residing in the British colonial realm. From then, Zoroastrians moved to other continents, primarily Britain, America, and Australia, where they now have intermittent communities. Zoroastrianism is recognized as a minority religion in India, Iran, Iraqi Kurdistan, the United States, Azerbaijan, and Uzbekistan. The Zoroastrian population is now sparse and distributed over the globe.

COUNTRY	ESTIMATED ZOROASTRIAN POPULATION
India	61,000
Iran	15,000–25,271

COUNTRY	ESTIMATED ZOROASTRIAN POPULATION
Iraqi Kurdistan/ Iraq	15,000
United States	14,405
Uzbekistan	7,000
Canada	6,442
United Kingdom	5,500
Tajikistan	2,700
Australia	2,577
Arab States of the Persian Gulf	1,900
Pakistan	1,675
New Zealand	1,231
Other countries in Europe	500
Other countries in Central Asia	500
Singapore	372
Hong Kong	204

After Zoroastrianism obtained official recognition there in 2015, three Zoroastrian temples were opened in the Kurdistan Region of Iraq. According to the local Zoroastrian community, thousands of people in the territory have recently converted to Zoroastrianism. Since 2014, more than 15,000 members have enrolled with the Yasna Association, a Zoroastrian advocacy group in the Kurdistan Region, according to claims made in 2020. The Yasna Association also serves as a spokesperson for the faith within the Iraqi Kurdish administration. In a 2020 online survey by the Group for Analyzing and Measuring Opinions in Iran (GAMAAN) that looked at Iranian people's attitudes about religion, 7.7% of the respondents identified as Zoroastrians. Significant conversions from Islam to Zoroastrianism have been reported recently in Iran.

FEZANA (the Federation of Zoroastrian Associations of North America) released a demographic profile of Zoroastrians worldwide in 2012, along with a comparison to a prior poll from 2004. According to a FEZANA survey, Iran and India are home to roughly half of the world's 111,691 – 121,962 Zoroastrians. According to FEZANA's estimation, 124,953 Zoroastrians lived worldwide in 2004.

ZOROASTRIAN INFLUENCE ON POPULAR CULTURE

Zoroastrianism and its ideas may be more familiar to you than you think. One can find the influence of Zoroastrian ideas and beliefs throughout popular culture in some of the most unexpected places.

In the 19th century, Friedrich Nietzsche wrote a book called "Thus Spoke Zarathustra," which introduced many Europeans to Zarathustra and the Zoroastrian religion. In the book, Nietzsche travels with the prophet Zarathustra. Given that Nietzsche was an outspoken atheist, some have considered the work an ironic portrayal of religion and religion in general. The book has widely been viewed as anti-Zoroastrian because many of the concepts he puts forth speak against monotheism and deny the dualism of good and evil that is so distinctive of Zoroastrianism.

Regardless, the book inspired a musical work by Richard Straus, who composed a piece for orchestra in 1896 with the same title. Although not many will have heard that orchestral composition in its entirety, the opening fanfare, called "Sunrise," may be highly familiar as it was used extensively in Stanley Kubrick's 2001: A Space Odessey filmed in 1968.

Queen is one of the most recognizable and widely listened to British rock groups of the 20th century. The lead singer of this band, Freddie Mercury, was raised Parsi, and he reportedly took great pride in his Zoroastrian roots. When he passed away in 1991, a Zoroastrian priest officiated at his funeral in London in 1991.

The Japanese automaker Mazda Motor Corporation takes its name from the Zoroastrian deity Ahura Mazda. The business believed that connecting with the "God of Light" would "brighten the image" of their initial vehicles.

A Song of Ice and Fire, a fantasy saga written by American novelist George R.R. Martin, significantly influenced the HBO drama Game of Thrones. He took Zoroastrianism and invented the mythology of Azor Ahai. With the help of the fire goddess R'hllor, who Martin may have patterned after Ahura Mazda, the warrior demigod Azor Ahai battles the darkness in this scene.

Aside from these instances, Zoroastrian principles are still prevalent in many aspects of contemporary popular culture. Consider Star Wars and the ongoing conflict between the forces of light and darkness. The pursuit for knowledge and goodness above all else, trials by fire and water, and other Zoroastrian themes, as well as the priest Sarastro, are thought to be prevalent throughout Mozart's The Magic Flute.

Nowadays, the French clothing company Zadig & Voltaire comes to mind when the term Zadig is mentioned. The name's origin is undoubtedly Zoroastrian, even though the clothing may not be. The story of the titular Persian Zoroastrian hero, Zadig, who eventually marries a Babylonian princess despite many obstacles, was written by none other than Voltaire in the 18th century. Other Enlightenment philosophers also shared Voltaire's genuine curiosity with Iran, which gave rise to his philosophical story while being occasionally flippant and devoid of historical context. Voltaire acquired the moniker "Saadi" among his peers as a result of his deep appreciation for Iranian culture. The West-East Divan by Goethe, written in honor of the Persian poet Hafez, also included a chapter on Zoroastrianism. Thomas Moore also lamented the plight of Iran's Zoroastrians in Lalla Rookh.

The Book of Arda Viraf provided an excellent account of a visit to Heaven and Hell before Dante's Divine Comedy. But, could the cosmic Zoroastrian traveler's report, which eventually took shape around the 10th century AD, have been known to Dante? Despite the two masterpieces' obvious parallels, one can only guess.

However, some places make the Zoroastrian link more evident. Raphael's School of Athens from the 16th century depicts the Iranian prophet clutching a sparkling globe. Similar to the Clavis Artis, a German treatise on alchemy from the late 17th/early 18th century, Zarathustra was mentioned in a few works with Christian themes and was dedicated to them. Zoroaster was renowned as a philosopher, magician, and astrologer in Christian Europe, especially following the Renaissance.

There may be Iranian roots in many pictures, stories, and ideas that people incorrectly think are a part of Western culture. Even Satan is a Zoroastrian concept in the end.

ZOROASTRIANISM IN NORTH AMERICA

In North America, it is possible to find groups of Iranian Zoroastrians and Parsi people sporadically in many areas. Although there are times when the Iranian and Parsi Zoroastrian communities in the United States follow different schedules and rituals, since these communities are small, many also go to the same places of worship. Both Iranian Zoroastrians and Parsis in North America are members of the same national Zoroastrian organizations. Seminars, youth initiatives, and federations connect these two communities nationally and internationally. These encounters influence different forms of American Zoroastrian identities and communities.

Despite having a short history in America, Zoroastrians represent a significant turning point in the development of ancient religion as two distinct tribes and streams of the same ancestry come together on the same territory. Over time, these communities acquired several doctrinal, cultural, linguistic, and gastronomic variations despite fundamentally similar beliefs and practices. The majority of Parsis from the Indian subcontinent speak English and Gujarati as their native languages, in contrast to the majority of Persian Zoroastrians from Iran, who are often more recent immigrants to the United States and Canada. Today, the two communities follow various religious calendars and celebrate holidays that are just slightly different from one another.

According to historical evidence, Zoroastrians first arrived in America in the 1860s. Zoroastrian Cawasji Zaveri was a prospector during the California Gold Rush. A letter opposing slavery written by a Zoroastrian named Dosabhai Faramji Cama was published in New York's Evening Post in 1865. Two more early Zoroastrians are Pestonji Framji Daver, a Parsi who immigrated to San Francisco in 1892, and Rostam Kermani; the first recognized Iranian Zoroastrian who came to the country in 1926. Seven Zoroastrians from the New York region gathered at Phiroze Saklatwala's sitting room on November 10, 1929. It is believed that this meeting led to the founding of the first North American Zoroastrian Association.

Along with early political and economic worries, the 1900s' strict immigration laws limited the number of Zoroastrians who could immigrate to the US. Zubin Mehta, a conductor, was one of the most well-known Parsi immigrants of that time. In the 1950s and 1960s, a large number of Parsis started to immigrate to the US in quest of employment and educational possibilities. The Zoroastrian Association of America was established on May 23, 1965, by thirty Zoroastrians from the Chicago region. The Association's stated purpose was evident in their newsletter: "...it is now time for those of us in the vanguard of this movement to strategize on methods to protect our identity and heritage while fully participating in the American way of life." Even though the original organization disbanded a few years later, the Zoroastrian groups' goal was to aid a small religious community in establishing itself in a new nation.

ZOROASTRIAN GROUPS AND ASSOCIATIONS IN NORTH AMERICA

Initially, local Zoroastrian communities met in homes for social events and religious holidays, which led to the formation of informal Zoroastrian organizations in the United States. After the Islamic

Revolution in Iran in 1979, more Iranian Zoroastrians emigrated to the United States, and by the late 1970s, the number of these congregations had doubled.

In the 1970s, the Zoroastrian people formed the first official U.S. Zoroastrian Association and built houses of worship. The Arbab Rustom Guiv Darbe Mehr succeeded the Zoroastrian Association of Greater New York (ZAGNY) in 1973.

The Traditional Mazdayasni Zoroastrian Anjuman (or Community) and the Zarathushtrian Assembly were both established on the West Coast in the late 1980s, following the establishment of the Zoroastrian Association of California and the California Zoroastrian Center in Los Angeles in 1974. Californian Zoroastrians initiated a partnership between the Rostam and Morvarid Guiv Dar-e-Mehr on Jamshedi Nowruz in 1992. As a result, ZANC, also known as Zarthoshti Anjuman of Northern California, was established in 1980.

The Zoroastrian Association of Metropolitan Chicago (ZAC) was founded in 1975 by midwest Zoroastrians. On September 3, 1983, the Arbab Rustom Guiv Darbe Mehr in Willowbrook, Illinois, was formally inaugurated. About 20 years later, the Zoroastrian Association of Houston (ZAH) funded a new building devoted to the history and culture of the Zarathushti people. New Zoroastrian groups were also founded in Arizona, Kansas, Washington State, Greater Boston, Metropolitan Washington, New Jersey, Pennsylvania, and Delaware.

In addition to these well-established organizations, small Zoroastrian groups have also begun in many other American cities, including Detroit, New Orleans, Central Florida, and Canada's Maritime Provinces.

Every community in the United States benefits from the Iranian and Parsi Zarathustis. The community attends only a few annual events, but some organizations maintain specific calendars for the two populations. To unite the region, other organizations are making a lot of effort. To encourage communal religious holiday celebration, the Zoroastrian Society of Washington State (ZSWS) adopted the Fasli calendar in the state of Washington in 1994. The Zoroastrian Association of Metropolitan Washington, Inc. (ZAMWI) in Washington, D.C., started with a bilingual bulletin in 1989 and currently offers Farsi translations in all of its publications.

Even while the disparities are stark, they are starting to disappear with the next generation. There won't be any more Parsi Zoroastrians of Iranian Zoroastrians, one Zoroastrian in the Bay Area remarked; we'll just be American Zoroastrians.

Most Zoroastrian organizations in the United States and Canada have connections through the Federation of Zoroastrian Associations of North America (FEZANA). FEZANA, which celebrated its 25th anniversary in 2017, helps communities by supporting congresses, youth activities, religious education seminars, and original community-building initiatives which provide resources and a shared community space for Zoroastrians throughout North America. It also publishes the FEZANA Journal quarterly. In addition, numerous regular and special committees oversee its operations. By representing a community with various Zoroastrian theologies and being impartial on touchy or polarising issues, it strives to uphold the autonomous attitude established in its organizational constitution.

The Canadian Zoroastrian community is an essential and active part of FEZANA's membership. Some of the earliest Zoroastrian groups still in existence in North America are found in Canada. Three Canadian dar-e-mehrs exist at the moment, one each in Toronto, Mississauga, and Vancouver. American Zoroastrianism is already taking on a unique face, with Zoroastrian youngsters taking part in yearly events, including overnight camps, "Z-Ski" excursions, and the Zoroastrian Olympics. In addition, a Zoroastrian scout troop exists in Toronto, just across the border. Troop Toronto 100 was established in 1990 and is still going strong. Additionally, the community frequently congregates for Zoroastrian congresses, including the North American Youth Congress, the World Zoroastrian Youth Congress, and most recently, the North American International Gatha/Avesta Conference, which the Council of Scholars on Zoroastrianism organizes.

Several websites belong to this ancient religion, from simple ones that give an overview to more complex ones that teach the Avestan alphabet and offer sacred scriptures and translations. The Traditional Mazdayasni Zoroastrian Anjuman to the "reformist" Zarathushtrian Assembly are only a few of the groups and people whose websites and web pages are run by other websites that offer online dating services for Zoroastrians. Additionally, there are Zoroastrian discussion forums and message boards and "Z-mail," a unique email directory for Zoroastrians.

In America, Zoroastrians frequently go unnoticed. However, there is a small group with recent history on this continent, and considerable immigration has only occurred during the past fifty years. The Grand Canyon's 7,136-foot-tall "Zoroaster Temple" sandstone top had been the most overt link between America and the sometimes-ignored Zoroastrian faith up until that point. When the temple was named, there were no known Zoroastrians in North America; today, there are over 15,000 of them, with six U.S. dar-e-mehrs and several organizations and associations spread over the continent. For Grand Canyon tours, money is now provided by the FEZANA Zoroastrian Sports Committee.

The actions that American Zoroastrians do to combine two antiquated traditions and produce history include creating places of worship, founding organizations, and attempting to add their distinctive touch to the American mosaic.

MODERN ZOROASTRIAN FAITH

Particularly in India, where it is believed that the Parsis first settled in the ninth century, Zoroastrianism has endured until the present era. Reformists and traditionalists are today's two primary Zoroastrian schools. The majority of traditionalists are Parsis, and like reformists, they acknowledge the Gathas and Avesta in addition to Middle Persian literature. Both groups primarily derived their contemporary forms from 19th-century changes. A person must be born to Zoroastrian parents to be a Zoroastrian because they typically do not permit conversion to the faith. Some traditionalists consider the children of mixed marriages to be Zoroastrians, though frequently only if the father is a native Zoroastrian. As a result of reform, the faith has become more widely known, and ritualization has decreased. Because of these changes, the Zoroastrian faith is now viewed more as a philosophy than a religion in many circles. The Neo-Zoroastrians/Revivalists are notable exceptions to the rule that neither school of Zoroastrians exclusively comprises all Zoroastrians. Instead, they emphasize the idea of Zoroastrianism as a living religion and advocate the revival and maintenance of traditional rituals and prayers while endorsing moral and socially progressive reforms. These Zoroastrian interpretations are frequently focused on Western issues.

Except for the Vendidad, both latter schools have a propensity to centralize the Gathas. The Pundol Group and Ilm-e-Khshnoom are two Zoroastrian mystical schools of thought that are prominent within a tiny segment of the Parsi community. Theosophy greatly influenced them in the 19th century and had a spiritually ethnocentric attitude.

The Parsis developed a reputation for their erudition and wide-ranging influence in many facets of life starting in the 19th century. They contributed significantly to the area's economic growth over a long period; many of India's most well-known corporate enterprises, including the Tata, Godrej, and Wadia families, are headed by Parsi-Zoroastrians.

Records indicate that Zoroastrian Armenians may have continued to reside in Armenia up to the 1920s, despite the long history of Zoroastrianism, which finally declined with the arrival of Christianity. There is still a small population in Persia, Central Asia, and the Caucasus. In the United States, a sizable expatriate population has grown, primarily from Iran and India, with smaller populations in Australia, the United Kingdom, and Canada.

At the request of the government of Tajikistan, UNESCO declared the year 2003 to mark the 3000th anniversary of Zoroastrian culture, and there were special events held worldwide. During this time, those in power updated many of the long-held practices for the 21st century. For instance, the Tehran Mobeds Anjuman reported in 2011 that for the first time in the history of Zoroastrian communities in modern-day Iran and all over the world, women were allowed to become ordained as mobedyars, or women assistant mobeds, or Zoroastrian clergy, in Iran and North America. Because they have formal credentials, the women can do simple religious tasks and can introduce people to the church.

Wherever they may be, Zoroastrians strive to maintain active religious groups. Communities of Zoroastrians frequently host lectures, adult discussion groups, and Gatha study circles as part of social and religious events that support their identity. Additionally, they support programs that educate children about their religion and support youth organizations that unite the bright future that lies ahead of them.

ZOROASTRIAN VALUES

Zoroastrian values display themselves in how Zoroastrians around the world treat each other. When we look at various Zoroastrian organizations around the world, it is easy to see that they are primarily interested in making connections, education, conserving nature, and helping others.

Along with these beliefs, gender equality has consistently distinguished Zoroastrians from their other citizens throughout history. Men and women, in particular, are advised by Zoroaster to use their own unbiased judgment to decide whether or not what he, Zoroaster, says in the Gathas has a message that pertains to them. The fact that Jesus addresses both men and women at various points in the Gathas is particularly noteworthy because it suggests that both groups are contributing to the campaign to promote compassion and expel evil forces. The equality of address shows that both sexes are respected and that both are confident in their skills.

One of Zoroastrianism's core beliefs is the absence of gender bias, which is reflected in the way society is organized in later texts, the priesthood, and the wedding rite. The ability of a woman to express her opinions in front of her partner and have those opinions recognized as accurate was and is still a defining trait. In every way, the Zoroastrian woman has upheld her equality in society and, when required—and not always in the absence of her husband—has served as the head of the home. Women have made decisions regarding property sales, inheritances, harvesting schedules, educational options, potential marriage partners for progeny, etc., while a husband has been absent or in the case of widowhood.

As evidenced in the late Sassanian era, Zoroastrian women also held the position of queen. Since the opening of girls' schools for Zoroastrians in the early 20th century, women have proven their competence in every field by obtaining high degrees and employment in all fields where men have succeeded. Furthermore, there are documents from antiquity that prove beyond a shadow of a doubt that women were seen as capable and deserving to attend priestly college, to officiate and administer to the religious requirements of their communities. This is particularly notable when it comes to the priesthood. Following this long-standing practice, which has been restored in Iran after falling out of use for many years. Eight female priestesses were recently consecrated and are now present at religious ceremonies. It is therefore apparent that given the extent of gender equality shown in so many areas, it can only follow that men and women stand side by side when it comes to inheritance matters or other rights.

A critical strategy for uniting the community is to organize social activities. Many Zoroastrian organizations will hold celebrations for the whole community to partake in. Often, depending on the groups that make up the community, separate Parsi and Iranian celebrations will be held since they follow different calendars. For those who are not near a global organization like the WZO, resources can often be found at these organizations for finding like-minded people in your area and celebrating with those around you.

Giving children the chance to go to school is often one of the main focuses of Zoroastrian groups worldwide. They aim to provide not only primary education for children but also provide interest-free loans and educational funds for young adults to further their education since this is seen to strengthen the entire community for the next generation.

As well as formal education, most Zoroastrian organizations spend some time and effort educating their members and the public regarding what it means to be Zoroastrian and deepening the faith of those who may not have grown up in a Zoroastrian community. This also includes educating non-Zoroastrian spouses so that they may have a deeper appreciation of the religion.

Zoroastrianism is an environmentally conscious faith; some have referred to it as the first Green movement. The Gathas regularly refer to Mother Earth and the wonders of natural phenomena like the moon, stars, wind, and other elements. Zoroastrianism, which puts nature at its core, is based on the idea that human existence, the seasons, and the elements are all intertwined. A few significant Zoroastrian annual festivities that honor nature are the midwinter fire festival, the water festival, the Mehrgan harvest festival, and the first day of spring, which is also the Nowruz or New Year celebration.

All Zoroastrian religious rites that priests conduct must be prepared with sprouting green shoots, fresh fruit with seeds, a tray of seven dried fruits and nuts (lork), water, some bread, a fire urn, and a vase of flowers and evergreen branches that are all set out on a white cloth. The Nowruz spread is a little more complex, signifying how nature provides us with all the fruits and vegetables that improve our quality of life and keep us alive.

According to Zoroastrian ideology, actions speak louder than words and thoughts. For this reason, good order, or Asha, is to be respected in regards to the ground, the water, and the air. It is considered that a healthy environment is essential for the capacity to make intelligent decisions that result in action. Therefore, it is highly respected to drain marshy, soggy ground and sow crops there to make it fruitful and turn the dry area into productive land. The environmental sensitivity permeating the religion gave Zoroastrians their reputation as master gardeners who knew how to irrigate under challenging situations and how to produce abundance while others failed.

When a couple decides to get married, they are frequently advised to cultivate the land and that it is customary to plant trees after each child's birth and death. Above all things, actions in a healthy and well-developed society must reflect people's decision to walk Asha's path.

Zoroastrian organizations and Zoroastrian communities generally take care to look after the needs of the elderly and those disadvantaged. This can be in the form of providing food and shelter to someone who has lost their living space, purchased groceries or made a meal for retirees, or helping to rebuild after a natural disaster. In addition, farmers and other small business people are helped by the community when starting in many areas, and medical grants can be available for dealing with unexpected medical costs.

The Gathas warn Zoroastrians against being sluggish and lazy. Each person is responsible for working so they can enjoy life and relax with the fruits of their labor. The community is strongly characterized by its work ethic. One of the good deeds that Zoroastrians are asked to perform is encouraging others to share some of what would otherwise be only for themselves. It is typical to discover someone endowing a hospital, an elderly home, an orphanage, or a school in more industrialized areas and among wealthier families. Parsees are particularly renowned for this type of charity.

Today, endowments are also established so that after prayer for thanksgiving and remembrance, communities can come together in the local center for a meal. As a form of thanksgiving for a stroke of luck or the fulfillment of an earlier imprecation, candles would occasionally appear in niches at street corners. All these acts of charity benefited the community in varying degrees depending on the donor's financial situation. Giving to charity makes it more likely that the individual in question will be able to depart from this life with no regrets and proceed to the next life with a light and joyous soul. According to Zoroastrian tradition, the goal for life is to pass away as a Niknam—someone whose name will endure due to their goodness.

WORLD ZOROASTRIAN ORGANIZATION

The World Zoroastrian Organization (WZO) has members from 24 different countries and has headquarters in the UK. It is a registered charity in India, the USA, New Zealand, Canada, and Singapore, where it helps to provide advocacy, community, education, and assistance to Zoroastrians anywhere in the world. The organization was founded in 1980 by a group wishing to help displaced Zoroastrian people that wished to emigrate to the West. Soon, a worldwide organization was needed to keep the scattered Zoroastrian population connected.

As a charitable organization, the WZO has the infrastructure and resources to help raise money whenever and wherever financial assistance is required. They are committed to assisting Zoroastrians in need and working towards the solidarity of the Zoroastrian community. Through this organization, Zoroastrian people can connect with a network of like-minded people wherever they are in the world, as they help to facilitate networking events, gatherings, and activities that support the community. They actively ensure that Zoroastrians are fairly represented and that their voices are heard through media, business, politics, education, and diplomacy. The WZO also provides educational programming for both Zoroastrian people and non-Zoroastrians alike who want to learn more about the history of Zoroastrianism. Social programming and educational opportunities help to maintain a sense of Zoroastrian identity for those who live in a community where Zoroastrians are in the minority.

Hamazor can find interesting and educational content in their publication, and it is available online or in print three times per year.

Social activities are one of the main focuses of the organization. At their headquarters in London, many ceremonies, including initiations and weddings, are held, and most can be viewed online for those not able to attend in person. In addition, they hold festivals and feast days, and some events follow Parsi traditions while others follow Iranian traditions to accommodate both segments of society. They can also help to organize events in other areas.

WORLD ZOROASTRIAN CONGRESS

The World Zoroastrian Congress is a worldwide meeting of Zoroastrian people approximately once every four years in a different location. The goal is to unite generations, educate and foster dialogue, and form bonds to last a lifetime. The largest gathering of its kind, the World Zoroastrian Congress, attracts more than 1,200 attendees from 16 countries, even though it has only been held 12 times so far. The programming during the Congress features a compelling roster of speakers, including Zoroastrian religious leaders and clergy, academic scholars, community leaders and facilitators, and programs tailored to a variety of generations in attendance.

Each Congress is different and incorporates some of the host country's cultures. Each Congress also has a different theme with the idea of bringing common issues to the forefront for the group to learn and discuss.

The themes for the last three World Zoroastrian Congresses are:

- ➢ **2022** – Bridging the Global Zarathushti Experience (held in New York)
- ➢ **2018** – Together Towards Tomorrow (held in Perth)
- ➢ **2013** – Zoroastrianism in the 21st Century: Nurturing Growth and Affirming Identity (held in Mumbai)

WORLD ZOROASTRIAN YOUTH CONGRESS

The Zoroastrian youth of California organized a shared vision over 25 years ago. Their group included both Parsis and Iranian Zoroastrians to bring together youth from all over the world. The goal of the group is to discuss and define the present and future of Zoroastrians as a community and to lay the groundwork for the Zoroastrian youth to lead our community towards that future. This revolutionary movement gave rise to the first World Zoroastrian Youth Congress (WZYC).

Since then, a WZYC has been hosted every four years by a particular nation, with the Zoroastrian youth of that nation uniting to plan the historic occasion. Over the years, hundreds of current and future leaders of the Zoroastrian community have gathered at this Congress, which is designed for Zoroastrian youth between the ages of 18 and 35. It has given them a platform to create international partnerships and relationships and work toward addressing our community's challenges.

The Congress aids in preparing the next generation of Zoroastrians to define what it means to be a Zoroastrians in the growing demand for a solid and cohesive international community.

CHAPTER 6
PARSI AND ZOROASTRIAN CUISINE

With a frequent focus on celebrations and festivals, it is no doubt that food plays an essential role in Zoroastrian culture. In this chapter, you will find descriptions of a variety of commonly made foods, some originating from Iran and some from Parsi communities originating in India.

Rice and lentils or curry are the foundation of a traditional Parsi lunch. Ras is a stew made without coconut, while the curry is produced with coconut; typically, curry is thicker than ras. Dinner would often consist of a beef meal served with potatoes or other vegetables in a curry sauce. Most meals are accompanied by kachumbari, a sour onion-cucumber salad. The classic Parsi egg dishes, such as the pora and the akuri (scrambled eggs with spices), are also well-liked among Parsis but less so outside of the community. Eggs are frequently prepared with vegetables, including okra, tomato, potato, and others.

In Mumbai and many South Gujarati villages, breakfast typically consisted of khurchan, offal meats cooked with potatoes in a spicy sauce, and some version of the ubiquitous deep-fried, fried, or half-fried eggs. This meal would typically be served with massive amounts of coconut milk that was frequently taken straight off the tree in rural settings.

Although it was long believed that vegetables were only found in the "diets of the poor," there is currently a trend toward vegetarianism, light eating, and even the avoidance of red meat.

Desserts that are common on holidays include vermicelli, sweet semolina pudding, and malido. Other popular foods include faluda and kulfi, adapted from the Iranian and Persian-speaking cultures' cuisine. At wedding feasts, lagan nu custard is a frequently presented delicacy. Bhakhra, a type of deep-fried sweet dough, batasa, doodh na puff, and khaman na ladva are all famous Parsi sweets.

Depending on the recipe, Parsis frequently use white sugar, cane, or palm sugar that hasn't been processed. Additionally, they have the Parsi garam masala, sambhar masala, and dhansak masala, three common spices that are frequently used in Parsi recipes. Many urban households utilize them in their food even though they don't always create them from scratch. Coconuts have made their way into Parsi ceremonial life and diet because they were regarded as exotic in ancient Persia. Dried red chilies, fresh green chilies, coconut milk, ginger-garlic paste, and tamarind juice are additional essential ingredients. The flavors of sweet and sour, and spicy are all mixed in Parsi cuisine.

When invited to a dinner party at an Iranian house, you can expect to see a variety of grilled or braised meats and hearty stews on offer, often spiced with very fragrant but mildly spicy ingredients with mountains of steaming rice. However, on Nowruz proper, you may look forward to a few dishes that are particular to the event. Typically, a herbed rice dish with some whitefish is the main course for such a feast.

Iran's geographic position makes it easy to understand why the range of regional specialties is so vast. The old administrative headquarters of the Persian Empire, Iran, has borders with Turkey, Afghanistan, Pakistan, the Arab nations, and former Soviet Union nations. Iran is located in the Middle East, but due to its advantageous location along the Silk Road trade route, it also has strong relations with Europe, the Far East, and Africa.

A Prayer Before Eating

MIDDLE PERSIAN	ENGLISH
Itha at yazamaide, Ahurem Mazdam!	Thus, we honor Ahura Mazda here.
Ye gamcha ashemcha dat,	Who provided the just earth,
Apascha dat, urvaraoscha vanguhish,	Gave the plants and good water,
Raochaoscha dat bumimcha vispacha vohu.	And illuminated the whole good planet.

ABGOOSHT – CHICKPEA AND LAMB SOUP

One of the most classic Iranian dishes is abgoosht. Because it is typically served in stone crock pots, it is also known as "Dizi." Lamb and chickpeas were originally used to prepare abgoosht hundreds of years ago. However, the meal experienced significant changes later when new ingredients were introduced to Iranian cuisine, such as tomatoes and potatos. As a result, serving Abgoosht is a distinctive custom. Before serving, small slices of bread are put to the soup after it has been placed in a bowl. The remaining components are then mashed together and served alongside the broth, including the lamb, potatoes, beans, and chickpeas.

AKURI – CLASSIC PARSI EGGS

This meal is regarded as a staple of the Parsi morning. Eggs are combined with mild spices, such as garlic, onion, and cumin seeds. The eggs are scrambled and cooked until they just stop being runny, not too stiff. Once this is done, diced tomato and turmeric are added, and then they are served with bread and a sprinkling of coriander leaves. For a spicier version, green or red chilis can be added.

ASH E RESHTEH – BEAN AND NOODLE SOUP

This silky herbal soup has noodles, beans, and leafy greens like spinach and beet leaves. Atop the soup is the sour kashk, a Middle Eastern delicacy produced from fermented whey with a sour yogurt-like flavor. Mint oil, crispy fried onions, and sour kashk are the most common toppings for this soup. This soup is typically offered when someone is ready to embark on a long journey. The noodles, which were created in China and then transported to Iran, are thought to represent the different paths people travel in life. Because of its lucky contents, it is also offered during Norooz, the Persian new year, which falls in March during the spring equinox.

BAGHALI POLO - RICE WITH FAVA BEANS AND DILL

Rice can be easily cooked in Iranian cuisine by mixing butter and saffron, or "Chelo," together. But occasionally it is blended with other components and called polo. You may prepare polo using herbs, vegetables, beans, nuts, dried fruit, meat, and even noodles. The main course of the dinner is polo. When fava beans are in season and young and sensitive, as well as when dill is, this polo is especially delicious in the spring. The meal is frequently prepared with extremely soft lamb slices and is flecked with green dill and fava beans. It can also be provided with bone-in lamb shanks. Just before serving, add the saffron to the rice to give it a light saffron taste.

CHICKEN FARCHA – MARINATED CHICKEN

One of the most popular Parsi chicken dishes is chicken farcha. Deep-fried boneless chicken breasts coated with an egg and chili sauce mixture after being marinated in garlic, ginger, coriander, garam masala, and pepper. This chicken dish is served with the chutney of your choice as the ideal appetizer for a dinner gathering. It is a distinctive chicken recipe that is appropriate for serving as an appetizer at celebrations and dinner parties.

DHANSAK MASALA – SPICE MIXTURE FOR MEATS

Perhaps the most well-known Parsi cuisine is dhansak. It is a flavorful fusion of Persian and Gujarati spices and ingredients that serves as the foundation for the preparation of chicken, beef, and other key items. Although Dhansak masala may initially appear monotonous, it is worth the effort! It combines flavors from Gujarati and Persian cuisine and is a favorite among the Parsi Zoroastrian population. The mixture is composed of:

> One ounce each of dal chini, tamal patta, khus khus, laung, and badian

> ½ ounce each of shahi jeera, methi dana, phool pathar, and mustard seed

> One nutmeg, grated

> Eight ounces of sabut dhania

> Four ounces each of jeera and sabut lal mirch

> Pinch of mace

The spice mix can be used to flavor lamb, mutton, goat, chicken, or vegetables, and is served with rice or mixed lentils.

FESENJAN – STEW OF WALNUTS AND POMEGRANATES

This famous stew combines tangy pomegranate with chicken or duck and is a must-have on the menu of every Persian wedding. A thick sauce is created by simmering onions, ground walnuts, and pomegranate paste. Saffron, cinnamon, and possibly a small amount of sugar are occasionally added to neutralize the acid. Fesenjan has a distinguished past. Archaeologists have discovered inscriptions dating as far back as BCE 515 that detail the basic foods that the early Iranians consumed at the Persepolis ruins, the ancient ritual center of the Persian Empire. The main components of fesenjan, such as walnuts, chicken, and pomegranate preserves, were also present.

GORMEH SABZI – STEW WITH GREEN HERBS

The sour and herb-filled gormeh sabzi, which is comprised of herbs, kidney beans, and lamb, satisfies two Persian food demands. First, dried limes, or limoo omani, are used to season the stew in Farsi. These limes taste particularly potent, sour, and bittersweet, giving the stew a distinctive flavor. The other element of gormeh sabzi that never changes is fenugreek leaves, which offer a flavor uncommon to most Westerners. The flavor of fenugreek is tangy, sweet, nutty, and slightly bitter. It is often compared to a combination of maple syrup and burnt sugar. Other herbs for inclusion in this stew are scallions, parsley, and coriander.

HALEEM - WHEAT AND MEAT PORRIDGE

The Middle East and Central Asia have long been fans of Haleem, a delicious, thick, calorie-dense porridge. It also goes by the names Harees, Hareesa, Keshkek, Kichara, and Daleem. Haleem's precise origin is uncertain. It is a star in Turkish, Arabian, Indian, Pakistani, and Bengali cuisine, although the recipe varies considerably depending on the region. Regardless of where it is found, wheat and meat are always required. To cook it, people utilize a variety of meats, including lamb, beef, turkey, and chicken breast. Persian Haleem is often eaten for breakfast and is slowly cooked for several hours, giving it a paste-like consistency.

JEWELED RICE - RICE WITH DRIED FRUIT AND NUTS

Iranian natural elements, including almonds, carrots, saffron, pistachios, candied orange peel, and barberries, are highlighted in this sweet-salty dish. Like little gems, it is sprinkled with vibrantly colored dried fruit and nuts. To counteract the tartness of the barberries, they are boiled with a bit of sugar. Because the sweet components represent a sweet life, jeweled rice is typically presented for important events, especially weddings. In addition, chicken is frequently served with it, and the sweetness goes well with the chicken.

KACHUBAR – CUCUMBER AND TOMATO SALAD

This is a fresh, easy chopped salad with a simple dressing. Although it is traditionally served with curries, it is often found as a side dish along with any meal. Tomatoes, cucumber, and red onions are dressed with lemon juice, salt, and a little cumin and chili. Fresh cilantro or mint are lovely additions as well if you want to add some fresh herbs. All the vegetables are diced into small, bite-sized cubes, and the dressing is added. For the best flavor, leave the salad in the refrigerator for a couple of hours before serving so that the flavors will combine and deepen.

KASHK-E BADEMJAN - EGGPLANT DIP

The Persian eggplant dip known as kashk-e bademjan is made with a few simple ingredients and is the ideal snack with some warm bread. The dairy product yogurt whey, which is made from drained yogurt and has a salty, sour flavor, is referred to as "kashk" in Arabic. Kashk can be purchased in a ball, thread, powder, or liquid form online or at Middle Eastern stores.

The recipe's main components are eggplants, kashk, onions, and garlic. Fried till golden brown are eggplants, onions, and garlic. They are then entirely mashed before being blended with the kashk. Given that eggplant has a propensity to absorb oil, additional oil may be required. The eggplants can be baked instead of fried if less oil is preferred. Blooming saffron, some dried mint, black pepper, and turmeric are used to season the dish. For extra crunch and texture, the dip can be garnished with sautéed dried mint, additional kashk, chopped walnuts, and caramelized onions.

KEBAB – GROUND MEAT AND SPICES

There are more kinds of kebabs than you can imagine. One popular variety is koobideh, which is ground meat seasoned with salt, pepper, and finely chopped onion. Despite how simple it sounds, the flavor is excellent. Kebab-e barg is a dish made of lamb or beef that has been thinly sliced, basted with saffron and butter, and spiced with lemon juice, onion, and other herbs and spices. Chicken kebab, or joojeh, is usually served with a whole chicken, including the bones, to add more flavor to the kebab. It is then basted with saffron and butter after being marinated in lemon and onion. Finally, Jigar, or lamb liver kebabs, are served with lemon and fresh basil leaves.

KHICHDI – RICE AND LENTILS

Khichdi is a rice and lentil meal that resembles a soupy pilaf. It is an easy recipe with a delicate flavor that can use any kind of lentils; however, masoor or moong daal is frequently utilized. The proportions of rice to lentils vary according to taste, but a 50/50 ratio is typical. The rice and lentils are cooked along with bay leaves, cinnamon sticks, cumin seeds, sliced onion, and ghee or butter and then boiled until the water has mostly evaporated. There are many ways to serve this dish, from butter and yogurt to fried onions, curry leaves, pickles, and tomato chutney. Add some potato, peas, corn, or carrots to the pot for more of a meal when the cooking time is almost finished.

KHAJOOR NI GHARI – DATES IN PASTRY

A delightful snack called a classic Khajur-ni ghari is made of maida-based pastries. The pastries are deep-fried after being filled with a sweet date and jaggery filling. The sweet date filling melts in the mouth as the crunchy, crispy, fried exterior tingles the taste sensations. Next, dates are minced, after which the mixture is cooked in sugar and butter until mushy and sticky. Add nutmeg, vanilla, and cardamom to the mixture to give it flavor. Before being baked or fried, tablespoon-sized balls of the date mixture are wrapped in dough.

KHORESHT-E BADEMJAN – TOMATO AND EGGPLANT STEW

The stew has a sheen of oil on top, a unique Persian culinary characteristic that shows a stew has been cooked long enough for the oils to rise and give the tomatoes a lovely red-gold hue from boiling with turmeric. The dish's moderate acidity, provided by the tomatoes, lemon juice, and occasionally the juice of unripe grapes, is balanced by the eggplant, fried till golden brown before being cooked with onions, lamb, tomatoes, and spice. Khoresht-e Bademjan is a thick stew typical of many Persian dishes and is best served with rice.

KOLMI PAPETO TETRALO – PRAWNS IN TOMATO SAUCE

Cooked in a sour and thick tomato puree are prawns flavored with chili garlic paste, chili powder, and turmeric. These are mixed with potatoes covered with salt, green chilis, and cardamon. In this hot Parsi dish served at New Year, shrimp and potatoes make up the bulk of the dish.

Serve with rice or roti, and be sure to save the shells of the prawns to flavor curries.

LAGAN-NU CUSTARD – CUSTARD FOR WEDDINGS

Lagan nu Custard is very popular to serve at weddings and is often called the wedding custard. It is like a Creme Brulee, made with milk, eggs, nuts, and cardamom. The custard is sweet, rich, and smooth and is always a big hit. The custard is made by combining milk and sugar and then adding cardamom pods and nutmeg. Often almonds, charoli nuts, or vanilla will be added. Sultanas are a common addition as well.

MASOOR DAL – RED LENTILS

Masoor dal is a tasty, enticing, and nutrient-dense side dish made from red lentils, spices, and herbs. This protein-rich dal is best served with cooked rice, millet, quinoa, or flatbreads like roti or naan. Given that they have a robust nutritional profile equivalent to that of meat, red lentils are a great supplement to a vegetarian meal. It would be best to soak lentils before being used in a recipe. After that, they are cooked in a pot with diced tomatoes and green chilies until they are soft. Turmeric, garam masala, bay leaf, ghee, garlic, and curry leaves are typical flavorings used in this meal.

PANEER CUTLETS – VEGETARIAN CUTLETS

Paneer cutlets are one of the most delicious, simple, and healthful snacks. Paneer is an essential source of calcium and protein for vegetarians. In addition, the cutlet can be used as the patty for a veggie burger. Similar to cottage cheese, paneer is an Indian cheese. These patties are made using paneer, mashed potatoes, bread crumbs, onions, cumin, garam masala, and turmeric. Vegetables can be added to the mixture if preferred. After combining the ingredients, shape the mixture into patties. Typically, the patties are pan-fried to create a crisp crust and then baked to finish cooking.

PARSI MUTTON CUTLETS

One of the most famous Parsi snacks is mutton cutlets, which are made by combining ground mutton and mashed potatoes with red and green chili, ginger, garlic, turmeric, cloves, cinnamon, and chopped pudina leaves. After being breaded and deep-fried, they are presented with a beautiful bowl of chutney and some thinly sliced onions. Parsi-style, succulent, and delectable mutton cutlets! This delicious snack is simple and quick to prepare and is perfect for any festive occasion or dinner party at home.

PARSI SALI KEEMA – LAMB MINCE WITH SALI

For a delicious Parsi meal, combine some lamb mince with turmeric, ginger, and garlic, and then mix with chopped tomato, onion, garlic, green pepper, coriander leaves, and mint leaves. The mixture is pan-fried and then served alongside sali (deep-fried potatoes). Sali can be purchased and is like potato chips. Alternatively, Aloo Lachas can be made by cutting potatoes into matchsticks and then deep frying them.

PATRA NI MACHI – POMFRET IN BANANA LEAVES

A seafood lover's dream, pomfret fillets are marinated in a mixture of salt and vinegar and then placed in a banana leaf. On top of the fish is added a chutney made from coriander leaves, fresh coconut, whole green chiles, cumin, garlic, coriander seeds, lemon juice, and chili powder. The fish and chutney are wrapped together in the banana leaf and steamed for 30 minutes until the fish is flaky and cooked through. This dish is often served at New Year and is extremely easy to make. If banana leaves are not available, then aluminum foil, parchment paper, or fresh corn husks can be used. Pomfret is often called Butterfish or Pompano in North America.

SADAB – RUTA LEAVES FRIED WITH BREAD

Even among Iranians, this meal is not particularly well-known. The primary component in this ceremonial dish is a vegetable known as sadab or ruta, typically planted in the gardens of residences owned by Zoroastrians. It is also planted frequently in the gardens of fire temples. The Ruta leaves are combined with mint and garlic before being fried in oil with water, vinegar, and turmeric and served with bread. This concoction is placed in a metallic bowl in front of the priest during Zoroastrian rites, particularly the yearly feasts known as Gahambars. One of the community members gives the food to the attendees after the ceremony is over.

SABZI POLO – HERBED RICE

A traditional rice dish often served at Nowruz (New Year) consists of layers of fresh parsley, cilantro, and fenugreek cooked in rice and garnished with saffron and a squeeze of orange juice. The dish is most often served with Mahee Sefeed, a whitefish found on the northern Iranian coast of the Caspian Sea. If Mahee Sefeed is not available, then any white fish, salmon, or trout can be substituted. The fish can be stuffed with pomegranates and walnuts or just with lemon.

Sabzi Khordan - Cheese And Herb Platter

A plate of sabzi khordan, or edible herbs, is essential to any dinner table. The plate is placed on the table at the beginning of the meal and left there throughout so that each diner can add herbs and flavor to their meal or partake of a palate cleanser when they wish. The components of the plate differ, but commonly included are scallions, radishes, walnuts, feta cheese, naan, mint, tarragon, basil, and cilantro.

Sali Boti – Mutton In Tomatoes

B boneless mutton is cooked in tomatoes, onions, ginger-garlic paste, cumin, coriander seed, vinegar, and jaggery, a traditional product made from date or palm sap. Garam masala and salt are added to taste. If jaggery is not available, then a dark brown sugar or demerara can be used instead. This meal, which is frequently offered at New Year, is a perfect illustration of the Parsi people's tradition of combining fiery and sweet flavors. Top the dish with crispy potato flakes and coriander leaves, and serve with hot chapati, naan, onion rings, and mint chutney. Potato flakes, or sali, may be purchased or made fresh by deep frying potato sticks.

Sali Par Edu – Eggs And Potatoes

This dish combines two of the most fundamental components, potatoes, and eggs, to create a simple Parsi breakfast plate. You may buy sali or create it at home by deep-frying shredded potatoes. After grating the potatoes, partially boil them. Add salt and pepper after they have been deep-fried twice, and then break some eggs on top and place it under a broiler until the eggs are cooked. This dish is often served with baked beans and toast for breakfast.

SALI MARGHI – MASALA CHICKEN

A spicy masala is wrapped around tender chicken, and shredded fried potato tops it off. An ancient recipe called Sali Marghi has long been a staple in Parsi homes. Prepare this dish for lunch or dinner and enjoy it with naan. The masala is prepared by combining tomato puree with sauteed onions, ginger, garlic, garam masala, turmeric, and chili powder. Salted chicken legs and thighs are added to the sauce with cumin powder and a little water and simmered until the chicken is cooked through. This dish is often served alongside some sali or potato lachchas.

SHIRIN POLO – SWEET RICE PILAF

This dish is commonly served on special occasions, like weddings, as well as at New Year. With toasted nuts, dried fruits, and candied carrots, it is balanced between sweet and savory and is an excellent addition to any feast. Basmati rice is cooked with a generous amount of saffron, and then any combination of garnishes can be added. Usually, this will include candied citrus peel, raisins, pistachios, slivered almonds, cinnamon, or julienned carrots. Caramelizing the carrots and toasting the nuts give the perfect balance for this dish.

TAHCHIN – SAFFRON RICE LAYERS

Tahchin is a popular rice dish that includes rice that has been infused with saffron, some meat or vegetables, eggs, and yogurt. Depending on what is stacked with rice, there are many types of tahchins. The most popular dish in Iran is shredded chicken tahchin, followed by beef, spinach, and eggplant. The word "tahchin" accurately translates to "place at the bottom" and is named after the crunchy outer crust at the bottom of the dish.

TAHDIG - CRUNCHY FRIED RICE

Tahdig is considered by many to be the national dish of Iran. It tastes a little like a cross between popcorn and potato chips while having a delicate basmati rice flavor. The crispy layer of rice is on the bottom of a rice pot. (Tahdig is typically not included on the menu; you might need to request it.) There are frequently a lot of leftovers during Iranian family gatherings, but tahdig is the one dish that is never seen again.

ZERESHK POLO – RICE WITH BARBERRIES

Iranians love the flavors of sour foods. Although they have a similar vivid red hue, barberries are considerably more tart than cranberries. This classic rice dish contains red berries that have been dried and then rehydrated before cooking. A lot of butter is used for cooking the rice, which helps to temper the astringency of the berries. Persian cuisine uses a variety of ingredients to make meals tarter, including sour oranges, quince, sour cherries, limes, sumac, rhubarb, green plums, tamarind, lemons, dried limes, and pomegranate.

CONCLUSION

We appreciate your perseverance in reading *Zoroastrianism: The Complete Guide on the Ancient Religion of Zoroastrianism*. We hope it was educational and gave you the knowledge and skills you needed to accomplish your objectives, whatever they may be.

Whether you have read this book to gain awareness of this religion or to deepen your spiritual connection with Zoroastrianism, the goal was to give you some insight into how and why this religion began, why it has persisted for so long, and some of the challenges that Zoroastrian and Parsi people have faced along the way.

If you feel called to delve deeper into Zoroastrianism, seek out some of the available Zoroastrian community groups. Even if there is not one in your community, there are several online-based communities that you can join and learn from. Most of the larger organizations, such as the World Zoroastrian Organization (WZO) or the Federation of Zoroastrian Associations of North America (FEZANA), will be able to point curious people toward Zoroastrian groups nearby or will have instruction and rituals available online.

In essence, Zoroastrianism is a faith that encourages people to live in a way that embraces the threefold path. Each person is reminded to live in a way that emphasizes good deeds, good thoughts, and good words. Establishing a community of like-minded people is an essential part of the Zoroastrian's path; honoring the spiritual equality of men and women and helping others is a daily way of life. By spreading charity and helping those less fortunate, the faithful can keep their souls aligned with Asha and spread happiness throughout their community. The core principles of Zoroastrianism instruct adherents to do good deeds without hoping or expecting compensation, notwithstanding the final reward of a seat in heaven.

Finally, a review on Amazon is always welcomed if you find this book to be helpful in any way.

A Prayer Praising Ahura Mazda's Wonderful Creations

MIDDLE PERSIAN	ENGLISH
Yazamaide ve amesha spenta, yasamaide haptan-gha-toish Handata.	In seven-chapter prayers, we honor and praise the eternally holy commandments.
Apamcha khao yazamaide,	We respect the water springs,
Apamcha peretush yazamaide.	We venerate the bridge over waters,
Pathamcha vicharanao yazamaide, Pathamcha hanjamanao yazamaide.	We forks in the roads and the intersection of the roads.
Gairish-cha afshta-chino yazamaide,	We give thanks for the waterfall that emerges from the mountains.
Vairishcha awezh-dana-ongho yazamaide.	We give the lake waters honor.

MIDDLE PERSIAN	ENGLISH
Aspenacha yevino yazamaide,	We laud the grains that are growing.
Payushcha thworesh-tara yazamaide.	We give thanks to those who cultivate and maintain the crops.
Mazdamcha Zarathush-tremcha yazamaide.	We thank the sky and the ground.
Zamcha asmanemcha yazamaide.	We praise the sky and the earth.
Vatemcha dare-shim Mazda-dhatem yazamaide.	We thank Ahura Mazda for the powerful wind he has produced.
Tae-remcha harai-thyao berezo yazamaide.	We laud Mount Hariti's summit.
Bumimcha vispacha vohu yazamaide.	We thank the earth for all of its blessings.
Apamcha frakhshao-strem yazamaide.	We adore the seas in motion.
Vayamcha fra-frao-threm yazamaide.	We honor birds' ability to fly.
Atha-uru-namcha paiti-ajathrem yazamaide, Yoi yeya durat asho-isho dakhyunam.	We admire priests who go to other nations to spread righteousness upon their return.
Vispascha Ameshan Spentan yasamaide.	All of the timeless, divine laws are revered.